W9-AZM-153

Life Under Soviet Communism

Charles W. Carey, *Book Editor*

Daniel Leone, *President*
Bonnie Szumski, *Publisher*
Scott Barbour, *Managing Editor*
David M. Haugen, *Series Editor*

San Diego • Detroit • New York • San Francisco • Cleveland
New Haven, Conn. • Waterville, Maine • London • Munich

For more information, contact
Greenhaven Press
27500 Drake Rd.
Farmington Hills, MI 48331-3535
Or you can visit our Internet site at http://www.gale.com

LIBRARY OF CONGRESS CATALOGING-IN-PUBLICATION DATA

Life under Soviet Communism / Charles W. Carey, book editor.
p. cm. — (History firsthand)
Includes bibliographical references and index.
ISBN 0-7377-1657-6 (pbk. : alk. paper) — ISBN 0-7377-1656-8 (lib. : alk. paper)
1. Soviet Union—Social conditions. I. Carey, Charles W. II. Series.
HN523 .L444 2003
306'.0947—dc21 2002035385

Printed in the United States of America

Contents

Chapter 2: Making a Home

Chapter 3: Getting an Education

Foreword

In his preface to a book on the events leading to the Civil War, Stephen B. Oates, the historian and biographer of Abraham Lincoln, John Brown, and other noteworthy American historical figures, explained the difficulty of writing history in the traditional third-person voice of the biographer and historian. "The trouble, I realized, was the detached third-person voice," wrote Oates. "It seemed to wring all the life out of my characters and the antebellum era." Indeed, how can a historian, even one as prominent as Oates, compete with the eloquent voices of Daniel Webster, Abraham Lincoln, Harriet Beecher Stowe, Frederick Douglass, and Robert E. Lee?

Oates's comment notwithstanding, every student of history, professional and amateur alike, can name a score of excellent accounts written in the traditional third-person voice of the historian that bring to life an event or an era and the people who lived through it. In *Battle Cry of Freedom*, James M. McPherson vividly re-creates the American Civil War. Barbara Tuchman's *The Guns of August* captures in sharp detail the tensions in Europe that led to the outbreak of World War I. Taylor Branch's *Parting the Waters* provides a detailed and dramatic account of the American Civil Rights Movement. The study of history would be impossible without such guiding texts.

Nonetheless, Oates's comment makes a compelling point. Often the most convincing tellers of history are those who lived through the event, the eyewitnesses who recorded their firsthand experiences in autobiographies, speeches, memoirs, journals, and letters. The Greenhaven Press History Firsthand series presents history through the words of first-person narrators. Each text in this series captures a significant historical era or event—the American Civil War, the

Great Depression, the Holocaust, the Roaring Twenties, the 1960s, the Vietnam War. Readers will investigate these historical eras and events by examining primary-source documents, authored by chroniclers both famous and little known. The texts in the History Firsthand series comprise the celebrated and familiar words of the presidents, generals, and famous men and women of letters who recorded their impressions for posterity, as well as the statements of the ordinary people who struggled to understand the storm of events around them—the foot soldiers who fought the great battles and their loved ones back home, the men and women who waited on the breadlines, the college students who marched in protest.

The texts in this series are particularly suited to students beginning serious historical study. By examining these firsthand documents, novice historians can begin to form their own insights and conclusions about the historical era or event under investigation. To aid the student in that process, the texts in the History Firsthand series include introductions that provide an overview of the era or event, timelines, and bibliographies that point the serious student toward key historical works for further study.

The study of history commences with an examination of words—the testimony of witnesses who lived through an era or event and left for future generations the task of making sense of their accounts. The Greenhaven Press History Firsthand series invites the beginner historian to commence the process of historical investigation by focusing on the words of those individuals who made history by living through it and recording their experiences firsthand.

Introduction

The rise and fall of Soviet communism is one of the most amazing stories in human history. As historian Walter Laqueur has noted, "to dismiss [Soviet] communism as if it were never of consequence shows neither good sense nor historical understanding."[1] Under leaders such as Vladimir Lenin, Nikita Khrushchev, and Mikhail Gorbachev, Soviet communism demonstrated the capability of making life significantly better for the average Soviet citizen. Under the notorious Josef Stalin, it created a society that was long on fear and repression and short on personal initiative and material goods. Under Leonid Brezhnev, Yuri Andropov, and Konstantin Chernenko, it established a system that seemed not to care about its citizens at all.

The Birth of Soviet Communism

Soviet communism was born in 1917 when the Bolsheviks, a group of Russian socialists, seized control of the Russian government. Earlier that same year, Tsar Nicholas II had abdicated the throne, thus ending the three-hundred-year reign of the Romanov dynasty. The immediate cause was the disastrous war effort against the Central Powers that had destroyed Russia's ability and will to participate further in World War I. The long-term cause was the tsars' inability to adapt to the social and economic changes taking place in Europe in the wake of industrialization. Following Nicholas's abdication, a provisional government had been established to rule in his stead. This government was a hodgepodge of competing factions, among them the Bolsheviks, whose constant bickering made it impossible for the provisional government to establish its legitimacy. Meanwhile, the Central Power armies of Germany and Austria continued to campaign on Russian soil, bread was becoming increasingly scarce, and millions of peasants were demanding a more equitable distribution of land than had existed under the Russian monarchy.

The Bolsheviks were able to take charge mostly because they were led by an extraordinary individual, Vladimir I. Lenin. According to Robert Service, a Lenin biographer, Lenin despised "every social prop of the tsarist political order. He detested the whole Romanov family, the aristocracy, the clergy, the police and the high command. He hated . . . the middle class."[2] His hatred led him to destroy the entire tsarist system. In its place, notes William B. Husband, he worked to bring about "a fundamental transformation of not only social institutions, but also values, myths, norms, mores, aesthetics, popular images, and traditions . . . nothing less than the recasting of the human condition."[3]

Of all the contenders for power in post-tsarist Russia, only Lenin had a clear vision of what the future should look like. This vision was socialism, as expounded by Karl Marx and elaborated upon by Lenin and other Russian socialists. The resulting political philosophy became known as Marxism-Leninism. Almost immediately upon taking power, Lenin engineered a peace treaty with the Central Powers that took Russia out of World War I. Then he began transforming Russia, one of Europe's last bastions of conservatism, into the Soviet Union, Europe's first socialist state.

The Influence of Lenin

Lenin's efforts to build socialism in Russia were impeded by the Russian Civil War (1918–1920) and his death in 1924. Nevertheless, he laid the groundwork for a number of the institutions that will forever be associated with communism. His most important contribution was to develop the idea of the hybrid party-state. Almost immediately after taking charge, the Bolsheviks began asserting their authority over the soviets (local councils), factory committees, trade unions, co-operatives, professional associations, and other bodies that had been providing local government since the tsar's fall. In time, the Communist Party emerged as the real power behind government.

Lenin created a secret police force to deal harshly with the enemies of socialism. Known as the Cheka, this force was modeled on the tsarist police and eventually transformed into the KGB, a political police and security agency. It was comparable in terms of its power and duties to the FBI, CIA, Secret Service, U.S. Border Patrol, and Immigration and Naturalization Service combined. In order to provide the peasants with some redress of their grievances over land distribution, Lenin established the first of the large collective farms that would become the mainstay of Soviet agriculture. His idea that non-Russian territories should enjoy some degree of autonomy in a Russian-led union resulted in the formation in 1922 of the Union of Soviet Socialist Republics (USSR), better known as the Soviet Union.

Lenin's unique ideas about virtually every aspect of Russian society were eventually incorporated into the fabric of Soviet life. His belief that the role of education in a socialist society was to impart practical knowledge came to life as the "unified labor school," which revolved around science and technology while stressing academic specialization and hands-on experience. His sense that the power of the Russian Orthodox Church, one of the main bolsters of the tsars' authority, had to be curtailed led to its disestablishment. His notion that women must help men build socialism, but could do so only after being freed from the strictures of bourgeois morality, led to secularized marriages, liberal divorce and abortion laws, and equal opportunity for women in work and society.

Stalin Takes Command

Upon his death, Lenin was succeeded as general secretary of the Communist Party by Josef Stalin. For thirty years (1924–1953) Stalin oversaw the evolution of Marxism-Leninism into what is now known as Stalinism. Stalinism was responsible for the complete transformation of the Soviet Union's economy, politics, society, and culture, and for its development into one of the world's superpowers via a program of rapid industrialization. It was also responsible, however, for the deaths of millions of Soviet citizens who perished while Stalin's plans were being brought to fruition. As historian Stephen F. Cohen contends, "Stalinism was not simply nationalism, bureaucratization, absence of democracy, censorship, [and] police repression, . . . Stalinism was excess, extraordinary extremism, in each."[4]

Prior to Stalin, socialist theory held that the fall of capitalism was imminent, and that the Soviet Union should serve as the vanguard for worldwide socialist revolution. Stalin rejected this notion in favor of what became known as "socialism in one country." He knew that righting the sorry state of affairs within his own nation would require all the efforts and resources available to Soviet communists. To Stalin's mind, it was much more likely that the capitalist countries would attempt to crush Soviet communism long before Soviets would be ready to export communism. He recalled that the West had invaded Russia during the Napoleonic wars in the 1810s, the Crimean War in the 1850s, and World War I in the 1910s, and had stationed troops in Russia in the 1920s during the Russian Revolution. There was no doubt in his mind that the next invasion was not far off. Indeed, he was correct; in the 1940s, during World War II, the invading forces of Nazi Germany and its allies inflicted tremendous suffering on the Soviets.

The Five-Year Plans

Defending Russia against the West meant embarking on a program of rapid industrialization. The vehicles for this program were the Five-Year Plans, the first of which went into effect in 1928. The first Five-Year Plan (1928–1932) called for a quadrupling of heavy industry and an increase in the output of consumer goods. In order to fulfill the plan, the Communist Party imposed strict controls over the Soviet economy. Before the plan's implementation, managers of state-owned enterprises produced for the marketplace as they saw fit. Afterwards, managers produced what the state planning commission told them to produce. Trade unions were transformed from organizations that protected workers into glorified cheerleading squads that promoted productivity. The small factories and businesses that had survived the first decade of communism were nationalized, so that the state became virtually the only employer in the Soviet Union. Any resistance to these plans by workers or managers was met by immediate banishment to a gulag (prison camp) or by death.

The first Five-Year Plan was too optimistic, largely because the nation lacked trained workers, its extractive industries for producing raw materials were undeveloped, its transportation system was woefully inadequate, and the bureaucracy required for a planned economy led to waste and inefficiency. Nevertheless, major increases were made in the production of electricity, steel, and machinery, although in many cases quality was sacrificed for quantity. The second Five-Year Plan (1933–1937) focused on the production of consumer goods, while the third Five-Year Plan (1938–1941) concentrated on building up the military. Although both were plagued by the same problems as the first Five-Year Plan, they resulted in even greater industrial advances. By 1941, the Soviet Union had transformed itself from a backward, agrarian nation into one of the world's leading industrial nations.

Agricultural Reform

Under Stalin, state control of the means of production extended to agriculture as well. Reasoning that economies of scale applied to farming as well as to manufacturing, central planners oversaw the collectivization of Soviet agriculture. The land holdings of landlords and peasants alike were seized and reorganized into agribusinesses known as sovkhozy and kolkhozy. A sovkhoz was owned outright by the state, and its workers were paid wages as if they were factory workers. A kolkhoz was a collective farm. Self-governed by a board of directors, it sold its produce directly to the government. At year's end, the profits were distributed to the kolkhozniki in accordance with how much and how hard they had worked.

Most landless peasants welcomed the development of collective farming because it promised to bring about a rise in their standard of living. Kulaks, peasants who owned so much land that they employed hired hands, almost unanimously opposed collectivization. The lucky kulaks were rounded up ruthlessly and herded off to the kolkhozy; the unlucky ones were murdered or packed off to forced labor camps, never to be heard from again. As Soviet dissident Alexander Solzhenitsyn put it: "Like raging beasts, . . . abandoning all humane principles which had evolved through the millennia, [the Red Army] began to round up the very best farmers and their families, and to drive them, stripped of their possessions, naked, into the northern wastes."[5] Although no one knows for sure how many kulaks were eliminated in the drive to collectivize Soviet agriculture, the most likely estimate is between 10 and 14 million.

Unfortunately, collective farming worked better on paper than it did in the field. One of the major purposes of collectivization was to produce a surplus of agricultural goods such as grain. In addition to feeding the growing number of industrial workers, these goods were to be exported to the West in exchange for the raw materials and machinery with which to industrialize. In fact, it took much longer than anyone expected to obtain surpluses from the sovkhozy and kolkhozy, and for a while they actually produced less than had the kulaks and other peasants. Undaunted by the lack of surplus, Stalin ordered that farm produce be collected and exported anyway so that the drive to industrialize could continue unabated. The result was a massive famine that plagued the Soviet Union, particularly the Ukraine, in 1932–1933 that resulted in the death by starvation of at least six million citizens.

The Transformation of Soviet Society

The Five-Year Plans and the collectivization of agriculture transformed the Soviet economy, but they also transformed Soviet society. Industry needed engineers to grow, and the Soviet education system was geared to producing engineers, technicians, and scientists in vast numbers. Unlike a western "liberal arts" education, which attempts to teach a student a little about many things, the Soviets developed polytechnical education, which concentrated on teaching a student math, science, and trade or mechanical skills. As industry expanded, so too did the availability and the demand for machinists and skilled factory workers. Between 1924 and 1941, the number of Soviet citizens who made their living as industrial workers increased astronomically.

Rapid industrialization resulted in the construction of cities in the middle of nowhere, so that factories could be close to sources of hydroelectric power and raw materials. As in the West, the rapid expansion of cities caused a number of social problems. The worst were shortages of food and housing.

By 1941 the typical Soviet urban family lived in a one-room apartment. A married couple commonly shared their apartment with their children, including those who were married and their spouses, and in many cases with one or more parents as well. Cooking was done in a communal kitchen that was shared with neighbors in the apartment building. Bathroom facilities were shared in a similar manner.

Although families could usually obtain enough food to eat, many items were in short supply, and the process by which they obtained food was tortuous. Families were issued rationing coupons to ensure that everyone got enough to eat. The coupons had to be exchanged in government stores where the employees were often surly and unhelpful. After standing in line for hours, customers often found that the items they had come to purchase were not available. As author Sheila Fitzpatrick has observed, "people went round with string bags in their pockets, known as 'just in case' bags, on the off chance they were able to find some deficit [scarce] goods. If they saw a queue [line], they quickly joined it, inquiring what goods were on offer after securing a place."[6] They had learned to buy what was in stock and barter it later for what they needed or wanted.

Other ways to obtain food were from the collective markets or on the black market. One aspect of the collectivization of agriculture was that farm workers were allowed to raise gardens and sell the produce at the collective market. Although prices were higher than in the government stores, the quality was better and the supply was more certain. The black market offered virtually all sorts of luxury items, including foods and consumer goods, to anyone with rubles to spend. Despite repeated attempts to stamp out the black market, including making entrepreneurialism a capital crime, it flourished throughout the existence of Soviet communism.

The Great Purge

Stalin was not the first Russian ruler to repress his people. Under the tsars, Russian peasants endured a situation that was little better than slavery; they were not emancipated until 1863, the same year that Abraham Lincoln freed the slaves in the United States. Lenin borrowed the idea of a repressive secret police from the tsars, and used it to help secure the gains of the Bolshevik Revolution. Stalin, however, established a program of state terror that was unlike anything the world had ever seen; his "accomplishment" has been exceeded only by the Chinese communists under Mao Zedong.

The extermination of the kulaks was only the first step in Stalin's program of state terror. In 1934 he initiated a purge of the Communist Party that removed from power virtually every one of the original Bolsheviks still in office, most of whom opposed Stalin's plans. Eventually the purge included the Party's rank and file, the Red Army's officer corps, and the middle levels of managers and bureaucrats. The most common charge against the Great Purge's victims was "wrecking" or attempting to thwart the building of socialism. About one million of the "guilty" were executed, and another 10 million were sentenced to long sentences of hard labor in the gulag, the system of forced labor camps that played an integral part in the drive to industrialize. Their relatives were shunned by other citizens, and they often found it extremely difficult to obtain food, housing, and employment, despite having committed no crime themselves.

The result of the Great Purge was that Soviet citizens feared for their very lives as long as Stalin lived. The Great Purge eliminated virtually all opposition to Stalin's policies, and soon he was able to establish a system of totalitarian regimentation that governed virtually every activity imaginable. Education, philosophy, literature, art, and science were all put to work in support of Communist principles in general and the correctness of Stalin's line in particular.

Another result of the Great Purge was the rise of a "cult of personality" with Stalin at its center. According to historian Robert Conquest, Comrade Stalin "was built up with the most astonishing adulation as a genius not only in politics, but also in strategy, the sciences, style, philosophy, and almost every field."[7] Part of the reason for the cult's rise was the peculiarly Russian roots of Stalinism. For a thousand years, the Russian people had revered the tsars as if they were semi-divine, regarding them with a mix of adoration and fear. It is not surprising, therefore, that some of this attitude would transfer over to the Soviet regime, despite the underlying egalitarianism of socialist theory. By the time of his death, Comrade Stalin was seen as the solver of all problems and the redresser of all grievances, in much the same way that Russian peasants had regarded their tsars.

World War II

The most horrendous event in the history of the Soviet Union was World War II. The German armies were responsible for the deaths of 25 million Soviets; they also left another 25 million homeless and destroyed an untold number of farms and factories in their invasion of the USSR. It is a testimony to the remarkable power of communism's ability to work that the Soviet Union emerged from the war as one of the two most powerful nations in the world.

Given Stalin's dread of the West, and his conviction that the West was destined to invade Russia again, it is surprising that he did not see the danger that Nazi Germany posed to the Soviet Union. Even though the two nations had just collaborated on a partition of Poland and were parties to a mutual non-aggression pact, by 1941 the signs of a pending German invasion were obvious. The Red Army, which had been purged of most of its best generals, was caught completely off-guard when German troops crossed the border in 1941. For almost two years, the German Army threw everything it had against the Russians. One little known fact about the war is that, for every German who served on the Western Front, eleven served in Russia.

The Soviets responded with an amazing display of courage and determination. Men volunteered by the millions to fight in what became known as the Great Patriotic War, and women volunteered to take their places in the fields and factories. To keep them out of the hands of the rapidly advancing Germans, the factories in Russia and the Ukraine were dismantled and moved by train across the Ural Mountains and set up in fields in Siberia. Despite the lack, in many cases, of floors, walls and roofs, the relocated factories continued to crank out war materiel. In time, the Soviet advantage in population and industry turned the tide of the war.

During the Battle of Stalingrad (1942–1943), the Red

Army finally halted the German advance. Over the next eighteen months it drove the Germans back across eastern Europe and into Germany. Had the Soviet Union's allies not invaded western Europe at Normandy in 1944, and then met the Soviets in central Germany, the Red Army might have driven the Germans off the continent.

Postwar Stalinism

The last years of the Stalin regime were devoted to recovering from the destruction of World War II. Rebuilding industry was the top priority, and by 1950 the nation's industrial output had exceeded that of 1940. The collectivization process continued to evolve, mostly as a result of mechanization and the application of scientific farming techniques. And the Great Purge was repeated, albeit in a smaller way, when Stalin sought to eliminate from the Communist Party anyone who had been "tainted" by association with the West during the war.

Stalin also oversaw the expansion of Soviet power into eastern Europe, and the beginning of the Cold War. The creation of the "Iron Curtain" that cut off Soviet satellite nations from the West was actually a defensive measure; the next time the West wanted to invade Russia, it would have to begin its campaign about 400 miles further to the west. Western apprehensions that Soviet dominance in eastern Europe would lead to a Soviet invasion of western Europe led the West to view the Iron Curtain in the worst possible light.

By the time of Stalin's death in 1953, the Soviet Union had been completely transformed. Despite the devastation and turmoil of World War I, the Russian Civil War, and World War II, the Soviet Union had become one of the world's leading industrial and military powers, largely because of his leadership. It had also become one of the world's most repressive regimes, and its citizens feared for their lives.

Khrushchev and Reform

Stalin was succeeded as general secretary of the Communist Party, the de facto head of state, by Nikita S. Khrushchev.

The son of a pipe fitter, Khrushchev had once worked as a shepherd and a coal miner. His crude personality belied a sharp mind that got to the bottom of things in a hurry.

Under Stalin, Khrushchev had been head of the Communist Party in the Ukraine, and he was as familiar as anyone with the atrocities committed under Stalin's orders. Throughout his regime, Khrushchev worked to dismantle the "cult of personality" surrounding Comrade Stalin. He also ordered the release of many of the political prisoners in the gulag, and the restoration of their rights and those of their relatives. He reined in the secret police, renounced repression and secrecy as instruments of state policy, and relaxed censorship. He retained, however, the centralized features of Soviet governance that Stalin had created and that concentrated power in the general secretary's hands. And he allowed a cult of personality to develop around himself. Historian Merle Fainsod notes that at one meeting "one speaker after another offered effusive thanks for the personal guidance and initiative Khrushchev had supplied in every sector of Soviet life from foreign policy and the development of guided missiles to cotton growing."[8]

Khrushchev's experiences in the Ukraine, the grain belt of the Soviet Union, had convinced him that his nation's most pressing problem was agriculture. Despite the mechanization of the sovkhozy and kolkhozy, food production could not keep up with demand, and the nation continued to be plagued by shortages of basic foodstuffs. His answer was the cultivation of the "virgin lands," the steppes of Siberia and the Islamic republics that had never been cultivated. Reasoning that the virgin lands held as much potential as North America's Great Plains, he oversaw an ambitious project to turn the Asiatic grasslands of the Soviet Union into productive farmland.

As Leonid I. Brezhnev, Khrushchev's successor, observed, "Many things went wrong at first. . . . People were arriving in uninhabited areas; . . . and sometimes knew little about farming. . . . [They] were living in vans [camping trailers]. . . . There were no roads, bread and other foods were supplied to the local store irregularly, and other goods were also scarce."[9] Despite such initial hardships, Khrushchev's vision was rewarded with bumper crops during the mid-1950s. By 1958, agricultural production in the USSR had increased 50 percent.

However, several technical difficulties, primarily insufficient rainfall, were never properly solved by the agricultural specialists, and the productivity of the virgin lands gradually dwindled. Also, Khrushchev had insisted that, beginning in 1960, the sovkhozy and kolkhozy in the virgin lands give over millions of acres to the cultivation of corn, despite the insistence of the agricultural specialists that corn would not thrive on the steppes; they, not he, were correct. By the time of Khrushchev's fall from power in 1964, the virgin lands program was generally regarded as a failure.

Khrushchev worked to reform Soviet society in other ways, too. He was sincerely distressed that Soviet citizens had sacrificed so much for so long and had so little to show for it. He placed greater emphasis on the production of consumer goods and housing, and increased spending on education and other social services. He shortened the work week, raised wages, and gave workers the freedom to choose their own place of employment. He also decentralized economic planning by allowing lower-level managers more freedom to make important decisions. As a result of his initiatives, between 1955 and 1960 the Soviet economy grew faster than the U.S. economy.

One of Khrushchev's negative reforms was the renewed war on organized religion. During the Great Patriotic War, repression of the Russian Orthodox Church had been ignored in favor of more important reforms. But in 1961, Khrushchev set out to obliterate the church, and nearly succeeded in doing so. His anti-religion campaign also struck mortal blows at Judaism, Catholicism, and Islam, reducing them to near-invisibility by the end of his rule.

Peaceful Coexistence and the Cold War

Khrushchev understood that the Soviet Union, despite its rapid advancement under communism, lacked the resources and the systems to compete militarily against the United States in a nuclear arms race. Consequently, he pressed the West to adopt a stance of "peaceful coexistence." For his part, Khrushchev dropped the Marxist-Leninist rhetoric that war between capitalism and socialism was inevitable. Instead, he challenged the West to allow communism to develop, with the promise that, in fifty years, whoever was ahead economically and socially would get to teach the other its ways. The West responded cautiously to Khrushchev's overtures, and in 1959 the United States even allowed him to make a state visit. During this trip he visited Iowa, where he got the idea to raise corn on the virgin lands.

Ironically, Khrushchev's success at pushing peaceful coexistence was nullified by two major Soviet technological advances. The first was Sputnik, a satellite the size of a basketball that Soviet engineers put into earth orbit in 1957. In addition to beating the United States into outer space, the event also demonstrated, to the West's chagrin, the superiority of Soviet polytechnical education. The second was the development of a Soviet intercontinental ballistic missile capable of reaching the United States. This missile was similar to the long-distance rockets already in the U.S. arsenal.

The downing of a U.S. spy plane over Soviet airspace in 1960 was followed by the erection of the Berlin Wall in 1961. These two events marked the end of peaceful coexistence. Thus, when Khrushchev remarked "we will attend your funeral," meaning that communism would outlast capitalism because it was a superior system, it was translated in the West as "we will bury you," meaning that communism intended to destroy capitalism.

The Cold War almost got hot in 1962 during the Cuban Missile Crisis. Khrushchev had allied the Soviet Union with Fidel Castro, a rebel leader who had overthrown the Cuban government in 1959. In exchange for Soviet friendship and aid, Castro became a Communist. To protect his regime from the United States, Khrushchev attempted to deploy Soviet-made nuclear missiles in Cuba, a mere 90 miles from the U.S. mainland. World War III was barely avoided when the

Soviets agreed to pull their missiles out of Cuba; in return, the United States agreed to pull its missiles out of Turkey, whose border adjoins the Soviet Union.

Brezhnev and the Retreat from Reform

The failure of the virgin lands program, the reluctance of Soviet bureaucrats to decentralize, and the embarrassment Soviets felt because of the Cuban missile crisis resulted in Khrushchev's forced retirement in 1964. He was replaced by Leonid I. Brezhnev, who took over as head of the Communist Party, and Aleksei N. Kosygin, who became head of the Soviet state. Nominally, the two shared power for ten years, but in reality Brezhnev was the Soviet Union's top leader.

Like Khrushchev, Brezhnev had been one of Stalin's stalwart lieutenants. Unlike Khrushchev, Brezhnev had continued to admire Stalin's achievements, even after Khrushchev de-emphasized the cult of personality. Upon coming to power, Brezhnev restored Stalin to a place of prominence in Soviet lore. More importantly, he began undoing Khrushchev's reforms, which he perceived were what had gotten Khrushchev removed from office.

Brezhnev's counter-reforms were welcomed particularly by the apparatchiks, the career bureaucrats and mid- to upper-level party members. The apparatchiks had opposed Khrushchev's program of de-centralization because it diminished their influence and, in many cases, forced them to move from Moscow and its comforts to smaller, less cultured cities across the nation. Under Brezhnev, the apparatchiks were restored to their former positions of influence and permitted to relocate their offices to Moscow. And where Khrushchev had forced older bureaucrats and party officials to retire at a relatively early age, Brezhnev permitted them to remain in their jobs until they died, thus choking off future reforms. Playwright Ion Druta had one of his characters, an apparatchik, put it this way: "Then Leonid Ilich [Brezhnev] appeared. . . . We lived fabulously, quietly stealing, quietly drinking."[10]

Although Brezhnev permitted Soviet industry to turn out

more consumer goods than Stalin had, he also directed it to focus on producing war materiel in greater quantities than ever before. Under Brezhnev, the Soviet Union directed most of its technological research to military ends. By the end of his rule in 1982, it was generally believed that the Soviet Union had achieved parity with the U.S. in terms of planes, tanks, and ships, and was closing the gap in terms of nuclear armaments.

Stagnation and Decline

Unfortunately, the focus on building up the military resulted in the stagnation of civilian industry. Instead of planning for the future of their particular establishments, managers concentrated on fulfilling their short-term quotas in order to keep their jobs. This narrow focus minimized innovative thinking and locked civilian industry into the status quo. Meanwhile, the West was beginning to computerize nearly every aspect of its society. Before long, the western economy was benefiting from markedly increased productivity, and it began to leave the Soviet economy far behind.

Under Brezhnev, agriculture returned to its former position as stepchild of the Soviet economy. Modest increases in agricultural harvests were negated by poor storage methods and an unsatisfactory transportation system. The result was that millions of tons of food either rotted before it could be harvested or spoiled en route to consumers.

Most Soviet experts now agree that the 1970s was the beginning of the end for Soviet communism. During the 1950s and 1960s, the Soviet economy was growing at a faster rate than the western economies, and the government was making major progress toward solving the nation's social problems. During the 1970s, the Soviet Union retreated into Stalinism, albeit without reviving the worst abuses of Stalin's reign of terror. Instead of looking for new solutions, it insisted on forcing the old way of doing things to work.

The results were disastrous. Managers resorted more openly to bribery and corruption rather than to innovation and dedication to meet their quotas. Consumers looked increasingly to the black market as a means of obtaining food and other necessities. Alcoholism reached epidemic proportions, and brought with it an increase in spousal and child abuse and absenteeism. The birth rate dropped to record lows. Most ominously, Soviet citizens of every rank began to lose faith in the power of socialism to change things for the better.

Andropov and Chernenko

Brezhnev was succeeded by Yuri V. Andropov, a career diplomat and former head of the KGB. Andropov attempted to address the myriad problems facing Soviet communism, but his advanced age and poor health precluded him from achieving anything of note. His attempt to eliminate alcoholism by imposing prohibition simply made black marketers more powerful and helped fund organized crime, much as a similar attempt had done fifty years earlier in the United States. Following his death in 1984, Konstantin U. Chernenko was named to succeed him. Unlike Andropov, Chernenko was perfectly content to wallow in the status quo. He, too, suffered from poor health as a result of old age and died in 1985.

Gorbachev and Reform

Chernenko was succeeded as general secretary by Mikhail S. Gorbachev; at age 54, Gorbachev was the youngest Soviet leader since Lenin. Gorbachev understood that the arms race with the United States was diverting much needed resources from the civilian economy, and he moved boldly to bring the Cold War to an end. He also understood the severity of the basic internal problems besetting the Soviet Union, and he moved to correct them as well. Gorbachev's glasnost, or openness, policy exposed the system's faults and generated new ideas to reform it. Perestroika, or reconstruction, tried to reform the apparatus by which the government and the economy were administered. *Demokratizatsiia*, or democratization, tried to reduce the influence of the Communist Party by involving the great mass of people in economic and social planning.

At first, glasnost seemed like a breath of fresh air to the Soviet people. For the first time in years, writers and artists were allowed to express themselves more or less freely, without fear of censorship or imprisonment. The apparatchiks, however, never welcomed glasnost, partly because it exposed them to ridicule and partly because they saw it, and rightly so, as being dangerous to national unity. The Soviet Union was composed of fifteen republics, several of which had once been independent countries. An unintended side-effect of glasnost was to allow independence movements in these countries, especially the Baltic states of Estonia, Latvia, and Lithuania, to arise. These movements eventually spread to the other non-Russian republics, and the end result was the disunion of the Soviet Union.

Perestroika was also opposed by the apparatchiks. They resented the attacks it made on their special privileges and on the system of bribery and corruption that kept them in power. They also suspected that Gorbachev's real purpose in pushing perestroika was to make himself more powerful, and several of his reforms did exactly that. To counter their opposition, Gorbachev forced many of them into retirement and replaced them with his own people. Unfortunately, these new faces proved to be just as prone to corruption as the old one he had replaced.

Moreover, they found it impossible to implement the type of market economy favored by Gorbachev because they lacked a proper model. According to historian Richard Pipes, "they seem to have believed that the nation had stored in it a great deal of latent energy that would be released as soon as the shackles restraining and silencing society had been loosened. This belief accounts for the rather reckless manner in which they proceeded."[11] By undoing the planned economy without creating a market economy that worked, Gorbachev's people sent the nation's economy into a tailspin from which it never recovered.

Demokratizatsiia was a disaster from the start. It led to the founding of numerous informal groups, the counterpart of political parties in the West, which eventually felt strong enough to challenge the supremacy of the Communist Party. Opposition to demokratizatsiia split the Party in two, and for the first time ever the Communist Party did not speak with one voice. Bickering between the two factions prevented the Party from maintaining its leading role in managing the nation's affairs.

Done properly, Gorbachev's three-pronged attack on the deficiencies of the Soviet system might have rebuilt Soviet communism into a stronger, more viable force. Unfortunately, his reforms were not properly "sold" to the Soviet people, particularly the apparatchiks, whose support for any type of reform was essential to its success. Although he understood clearly the need to reform Soviet communism by making it more capitalistic and democratic, he grossly underestimated the difficulty of imposing these ideals on a people who had been taught for sixty years that they were evil. In the end, Gorbachev's reforms undid Soviet communism without providing a workable alternative.

The End of Soviet Communism

In 1991 Gorbachev was overthrown temporarily by a coup led by the old guard of the apparatchiks. Although the coup failed after a few days, it exposed the extreme weakness of Gorbachev's regime and led to his forced resignation later that year. By the end of the year, the constituent republics had declared their independence and the death of the Soviet Union. In its wake, the fifteen republics pursued various economic and political courses, but all steered away from communism. The grand experiment of Soviet-style socialism had come to an end.

Notes

1. Walter Laqueur, *The Dream That Failed: Reflections on the Soviet Union.* New York: Oxford University Press, 1994, p. ix.
2. Robert Service, *Lenin: A Biography.* Cambridge, MA: Harvard University Press, 2000, pp. 98–99.
3. William B. Husband, "The New Economic Policy (NEP) and the Revolutionary Experiment, 1921–1929," in Gregory L. Freeze, ed.,

Russia: A History. New York: Oxford University Press, 1997, pp. 280–81.

4. Stephen F. Cohen, *Rethinking the Soviet Experience: Politics and History Since 1917.* New York: Oxford University Press, 1985, p. 48.
5. Alexander Solzhenitsyn, *The Gulag Archipelago, 1918–1956.* New York: Harper & Row, 1973, p. 56.
6. Sheila Fitzpatrick, *Everyday Stalinism: Ordinary Life in Extraordinary Times: Soviet Russia in the 1930s.* New York: Oxford University Press, 1999, p. 41.
7. Robert Conquest, *The Great Terror: A Reassessment.* New York: Oxford University Press, 1990, p. 59.
8. Merle Fainsod, "What Happened to 'Collective Leadership'?" in Abraham Brumberg, ed., *Russia Under Khrushchev: An Anthology from "Problems of Communism."* New York: Praeger, 1962, pp. 97–98.
9. Leonid I. Brezhnev, *Leonid I. Brezhnev: Pages from His Life.* New York: Simon and Schuster, 1978, p. 118.
10. Quoted in Stephen Kotkin, *Armageddon Averted: The Soviet Collapse, 1970–2000.* New York: Oxford University Press, 2001, p. 10.
11. Richard Pipes, "The Rise of Gorbachev: Perestroika and Glasnost," in Paul A. Winters, ed., *The Collapse of the Soviet Union.* San Diego: Greenhaven Press, 1999, p. 90.

Chapter 1

Earning a Living

Chapter Preface

Westerners hold several misconceptions about the nature of work under Soviet communism. One is that the government told everyone what to do and where to do it. Another is that everyone got paid the same, regardless of what type of work they did. A third is that entrepreneurialism was strictly forbidden by the Communist regime. In fact, none of these was true.

It is true that most agricultural workers were organized into either collective farms (kolkhozy) or state farms (sovkhozy). Kolkhozniki, the members of a kolkhoz, sold their produce to the state at predetermined prices, while sovkhozniki were little more than salaried employees of the government. Even so, by 1935 members of both arrangements were permitted to work private garden plots in their spare time and to sell the produce legally at farmers' markets, where the prices were determined by the laws of supply and demand.

For nonagricultural workers, the labor situation was much the same as in the West. Most workers were free to move about the country, selling their services to whatever industrial complex they chose. In order to find employment in the Soviet Union, one simply presented oneself to the local labor exchange office (*birzha truda*). As in a Western employment office, the prospect's abilities were matched against the needs of various employers, the best possible fit was made, and the prospect was sent out on a job interview. Enterprising workers were rewarded by the system, with both higher pay and better jobs.

Because the Soviets made rapid industrialization a top priority, engineers were in great demand and were able to command relatively high wages and benefits. In some industries, factories actually competed with each other for skilled engineers. So great was the demand that even women were recruited and trained as engineers if they possessed the requisite abilities, something that, at the time, the West was reluctant to do.

Although entrepreneurs generally were not encouraged by the Soviet system, small business people who operated clandestinely were usually tolerated. This situation existed because the state economy was unable to meet the people's needs for consumer goods. As a result, the production of such goods was left in the hands of small entrepreneurs and a few small industrial collectives.

In terms of labor, the major difference between capitalism and communism had to do with political outcasts and their relatives. While such persons do not exist in the West, they existed by the thousands in the Soviet Union. Outcasts, usually men, were often sent to forced labor camps (gulags), where many perished. Meanwhile, their female relatives (*stopiatnitsy*), even those who had committed no crime, were legally denied the right to work, and many were forced to live from hand to mouth as best they could.

Hard Work and Initiative Pay Off

Yakov Alpert

One of the major differences between communism and capitalism in the early twentieth century was their conceptions of higher education. In America, college was open to all, but not all working class families could afford enrollment. Under Soviet communism, colleges preferred to admit the children of blue-collar workers, because they were considered most likely to build state socialism. As for employment, the two systems were not so different. Both ran labor exchange offices or employment commissions, although in the United States these were (and still are) operated by the states and not the national government. But in both systems "who you know" was always the surest path to a good job. Moreover, both systems rewarded hard work by paying higher wages to those who produced more or whose skills were in the greatest demand.

Yakov Alpert was one of the top physicists in the Soviet Union's space program and worked in the Academy of Sciences for fifty-five years. In 1987, he immigrated to the United States. In this selection from his autobiography, he discusses the rejection of his college application, his first job out of school as an unskilled laborer at a Moscow construction site in 1929, and how he later moved up to architectural draftsman. While showing how one got into college and found work in the Soviet Union, the selection also shows that hard work and initiative paid off under a Communist regime.

Yakov Alpert, *Making Waves: Stories from My Life*. New Haven, CT: Yale University Press, 2000.

I became an independent and self-reliant fellow when I was thirteen or fourteen years old, and I educated myself in many areas. At the Industrial Technical College I was taught the trade of carpentry and cabinetmaking. I taught myself another skill in those years, that of technical drawing, because I loved to draw and did it well. I earned a fair amount of money executing and copying technical drawings for people in Zhitomir. Although throughout my life I have enjoyed working with my hands, I did not want to spend my life as a cabinetmaker or a draftsman. I wanted to continue learning, working, and advancing my education, and to become a researcher in physics.

The only institute accessible to me for higher education, however, was the new one that opened at that time in Zhitomir. My friend Tolya Grinberg had the chance to go to the big city of Kiev for his education. His parents, who were better off financially than mine, were able to send him to the Polytechnic Institute in Kiev, one of the best and most famous of Russian institutes. Vladimir Zvorykin, the inventor of the television picture tube, the famous mechanical scientist Stefan Timoshenko, and the chemist Nikolai Uspensky were students at that institute. They immigrated to the United States in the 1920s and became prominent researchers there.

Refused Admission to College

I passed all my entrance examinations at the institute at Zhitomir with the highest grades, but I was not admitted. At that time the privilege of being admitted to an institute of higher learning was accorded only to the children of workers and peasants. My father was not a worker *(rabochii* in Russian); officially he was included in the category of office workers *(sluzhashchiy).* The rule was strictly followed in Zhitomir. It seems that in Kiev this was not so, because Tolya's father was also an office worker.

Soon after being turned away from the institute in Zhitomir, I decided to go to Moscow to be closer to the great world of science, to find a job there, and to pursue more self-education in libraries. I saved money for the trip from my drafting work; I even sold my precious photographic camera. I put the books of my library, some files and notes, and my collection of beetles in my parents' attic. I did not know what awaited me in Moscow, but I was full of optimism and eager to try my luck. . . .

Looking for Work in Moscow

It was the beginning of 1929 when I set out for Moscow with the few rubles I had saved from my drafting work. It was the first time I traveled outside Zhitomir. Although I had no definite prospects, I did have a lifeline in Moscow, my aunt Lisa, my father's sister, and her husband, Nathan Meyerovich. . . .

Aunt Lisa and Uncle Nathan opened their home to me. They lived modestly in two separate rooms in a large apartment that also housed three other families, with one kitchen and one bathroom among them all. Aunt Lisa and Uncle Nathan gave me a bed in the corner of one room, and Uncle Nathan made it his special project to help and encourage me. Nothing lit up this big-hearted man's broad, good-natured face so much as an idea for helping a relative, friend, or neighbor.

To find a job in Moscow at that time it was necessary to register at the *birzha truda*, or the labor exchange office. I presented myself there as an unskilled laborer. I cannot recall precisely why I said nothing about my carpentry and drafting or, more significant, my facility with electrical and radio equipment. It seems to me now that I was solely intent on learning physics in the library. I was ready to work hard, but I wanted free time to read. I was not sure that I could ever afford to become a full-time student.

In any event, the birzha sent me to one of the building sites of Mosstroy, the Moscow municipal construction authority, which was running major construction projects throughout the city. At the building site, I was hired to work on a building brigade, or crew, of unskilled workers. Of all the members of the crew, about ten to fifteen persons, I was the youngest.

Ten or twelve large buildings of several stories each were

going up on this site. Several building brigades worked at the site, all responsible for hauling in building materials, carting away refuse and excess materials, and cleaning dirt and debris from the finished areas of the buildings. The brigades were all paid the same base wage, 1 ruble 47 kopecks per day for each man, but the more a brigade accomplished, the

Workers' Wages and Benefits

Long-standing misconceptions concerning Soviet labor include the notions that workers were assigned occupations regardless of their interests or abilities, and that all workers were paid the same regardless of occupation. John Gunther wrote the popular "Inside . . ." series of books, and in 1956 he traveled to the Soviet Union to write Inside Russia Today. *This excerpt addresses those misconceptions by outlining the rights and rewards of the typical Soviet worker in the late 1950s.*

The first minimum wage law in Russian history went into effect on January 1, 1957. The wage differs depending on the location and type of industry. . . . The forty-eight-hour week was cut to forty-six hours, with two hours off on Saturday. . . . Pensions begin for men at sixty, after twenty-five years of service, and for women at fifty-five; the amounts range from 100 to 55 percent of salary; . . . workers now have the right to change jobs without permission; they can thumb a nose at a boss and quit, a privilege that did not exist before. However, two weeks' notice must be given. . . . Health insurance does not become effective until a worker has been at a post for six months, and vacations are tied to tenure. . . . Scale of pay depends not so much on what work a person does, but on the type of industry; if a particular industry is important to the state at a given moment, its help is better paid. A good deal is done to encourage incentive and productivity by way of bonuses, differential awards, and the like.

John Gunther, *Inside Russia Today.* New York: Harper & Brothers, 1957, pp. 370–71.

more kopecks its members received. Each brigade was responsible for recording its completed jobs on a list, which had to be submitted to the financial vice-manager of the site every two weeks.

As we worked outside in the Moscow winter, I gradually realized that my brigade only received the minimum wage, because no one on the team wrote well enough to keep track of the work we did. I started to write the jobs down carefully as we completed them. I gave the list to the crew leader, and our wages quickly rose to 3 rubles 47 kopecks a day. This was cause for celebration among the crew, and soon the news of our salary increase became the talk of the building site. The other members of the crew and the crew leader himself asked me to become the crew leader, but I did not want to displace anyone from his role.

With 3 rubles 47 kopecks a day, I could not only live in Moscow. A small loaf of good French bread then cost 5 kopecks. With 3 rubles 47 kopecks a day, I could save up to buy a ticket to the Moscow Art Theater. . . .

From Construction Worker to Draftsman

Early every morning from Monday to Saturday, without fail, I reported for work on the building site. One day a tall, handsome man strode onto the construction site. Everyone else knew who he was and deferred to him. A co-worker explained that this was Constantin Nikolayevich Chernopyatov, the principal architect of the project, on a periodic visit to check its progress. On this day he was apparently also curious to meet the young worker who was being talked about all over the building site. He engaged me in conversation and I found myself saying that I could draw well. He immediately asked me to come to his office the next day. There I showed him my drawing ability and told him about my desire to become a physicist. He then offered me a position as a draftsman. From the very beginning he gave me challenging work that was not connected with Mosstroy's construction projects. Chernopyatov was taking part in many architectural competitions, and he asked me to prepare the drafts and detailed axonometric views of his designs. Sometimes he gave me only a rough sketch, and from that I extrapolated elaborate, detailed views. I also began to accompany Chernopyatov to building sites, carrying plans and maps and a logbook for recording the progress of different projects.

Chernopyatov was delighted with my work. He even began to suggest that I should become an architect. He urged me to enter the Moscow Institute of Architecture, and I am sure that he would have helped me to do so. But although I loved architecture, I was even more interested in physics. And to become a physicist, I would sooner or later have to leave Mosstroy.

Making Ends Meet as an Entrepreneur

Mary Halasz

In theory, private enterprise did not exist under Soviet communism. But in practice, it thrived, often with the tacit approval of Party authorities. This was because the Soviet economy was hard-pressed to produce the heavy machinery and equipment required to modernize its industry, mechanize its farms, house its citizens, and defend its borders. And since this aspect of capitalism was tolerated, the public developed a desire for consumer goods, particularly clothing and gift items.

Mary Halasz was born in Czechoslovakia to Hungarian parents; as an infant, she moved to Roebling, New Jersey. In 1937, at age sixteen, she married Sandor (Sanyi) Laszota, a Hungarian teacher, and settled with him in Uzhhorod, a city in far eastern Czechoslovakia that was annexed by the Soviet Union after World War II. In 1949 her husband was jailed by the Soviets for fighting against the Red Army in the war, and she was forced to rely on her wits to support herself and their two children. This selection from her memoirs describes how she earned a living by knitting unique fashion items and selling them privately until she could find a "real" job.

After returning from L'viv [where her husband had been imprisoned on political charges] I had to find some sort of livelihood. Until then we scraped along with the help of friends. My friend Csöpike and her family, who were well off, invited us for dinner remarkably often. Mamuka also

Mary Halasz, with Piroska E. Kiss and Katalin E. Kiss, *From America with Love: Memoirs of an American Immigrant in the Soviet Union*. Boulder, CO: East European Monographs, 2000.

treated us to meals sometimes. Aunt Olga, who also invited us for lunch every now and then, related to her daughter living in Budapest what had happened to us, and her daughter Gizike wrote everything to my parents. Mommy found out how they could help us. She made a deal with Aunt Olga that they would support Gizike financially in Budapest, and in return Aunt Olga would provide us with dinner every day. So I only had to earn enough money to buy us breakfast and supper, which I did at first mainly by knitting.

Being Self-Employed Under Socialism

Knitted clothing was very easy to sell. In fact, I would knit to order, so I could count on knitting as a permanent, safe source of income. I discovered that more things could be unravelled and be knit from than anyone would imagine. For example, I unravelled the American flour sacks. Though the weft was made of paper, the warp could be used for knitting. It was not easy to work with, though, for it cut my hands and caused them to bleed. On the other hand, the beige-colored material was very easy to dye. I knit excellent trousers from it for the winter. I also used bandages cut into strips. I knitted baby jackets and baby caps with them. They were tousled and frilly and they looked cute. I also worked for peasant women from the country. They brought me their old-fashioned shawls which I unravelled and reknit into sweaters. Years later yarn reappeared in the shops. It was rather uneven, but it was pure wool. I realized that if I knitted with prewashed wool, the sweater would never change its shape. I knitted many, very many wonderful things with it!

One fall knitted and crocheted caps came into fashion. I looked at the most fashionable forms, did some experimenting, and then I started mass production. I showed the first sample pieces to my former colleagues in the National Bank. Each of them bought one. Then they also ordered mufflers to go with the caps. In the end, they even brought me the yarn, and I only had to do the knitting. By the time every woman had a cap, knitted hats came in, so I could begin to mass-produce knitted hats!

A friend of ours, Jóska, worked as the stockkeeper of the central iron wares warehouse of an industrial cooperative (the place where later I would also find a job). He was the one who issued the raw materials to the workshops. Occasionally I dropped in on Jóska and asked him for a handful of nails, or something else that I needed to solve some household problem. Once the warehouse received a huge consignment of waxed cloth. Several rolls arrived in lovely colors: red, yellow, brown, green, white, and black. Jóska had no idea what to do with them. No unit of the industrial cooperative used any waxed cloth. On the other hand, it did not occur to him—and it would not have occurred to anybody else—to return what he had been allotted. Everything was to be appreciated! Besides, a person who did not want his allocation was not given anything the next time.

A friend of mine had just been to Moscow, where she had bought a satchel-like red bag with a drawstring. It looked very good. I borrowed it, and took it to Olga, Jóska the stockkeeper's wife. Olga was very good at sewing. I showed her the bag, and asked her if, in her opinion, we could also make a similar one. She looked at it, and cut out the pattern immediately. We made a few test pieces of different colors and also lined them nicely. Then I put one on my shoulder and walked around in the city. Every woman I met stopped me and asked me where I had obtained that cute bag of mine, and if I could also get one for them. "I am not sure," I answered, "but I will try." And the news about the provenance of ladies' bags spread by word of mouth. Olga was kept busy for months, putting bags together. We used up the whole waxed cloth consignment of the warehouse. I received a decent percentage of the profits. Although I did not participate in the production, I was the creative source of the idea and I was the saleswoman. It was a product of unbelievable success, and it brought a nice income for both of us.

Before the Christmas of 1949, our first Christmas without Sanyi, we found another source of livelihood, too. In the streets young Gypsy girls were selling Christmas wrappings for candies to be hung on the Christmas tree. Lia looked at the wrappings, and came home with the idea that we could make much nicer ones. We tried, and indeed, we found that if we cut the edges while holding several pieces of paper together, then, when we pulled the sheets apart, the fringes became ruffled in a lovely way. We filled these wrappings with the cheapest sweets that could be bought and we had unbelievable success with them! We did nothing else for a whole week, and just could not make enough of them. To tell the truth, the paper for the wrappings came from the office of the cooperative. After we had been robbed by the State of everything we had, including the head of the family, I stopped having qualms about using up a little waxed cloth, a few nails, or some paper from the common property. We lived as we could. One sheet of paper was sufficient for two wrappings. They were so beautiful that not even today's Christmas wrappings could match them. We also presented our friends with sweets in Christmas wrappings. We made a boxful for each of them.

Working in a Cooperative

I also had extra income after I found regular work, thanks to my boss. There was a shortage of handkerchiefs in the city, and our cooperative decided to manufacture them. The handkerchiefs were cut and edged by a team of three. One of the paints available resisted washing fairly well; it did not fade. We used this paint to stripe the handkerchiefs by hand with a pipette. They let me have a bunch of handkerchiefs to stripe at home. This, naturally, meant that I did not sleep because I spent half of every night pipetting. The reasonable thing to do would have been to stripe as many handkerchiefs as possible in the shortest possible time, instead, I let my imagination run free and I kept changing the pattern, also because that way it was less boring. Little Lia also prepared lovely designs: different combinations of colors, of wide and narrow stripes, etc. We kept making them more and more beautiful until the others got fed up that only our handkerchiefs had any success. So my career as a handkerchief-decorator came to an end, but while it lasted, it meant good income. That was the way we lived, always embracing every opportunity we could.

It took me a lot of time and effort to find a regular job. Bosses tried to avoid employing prisoners' wives. The cooperative where I found work eventually was managed by a sweet Jewish man who did not forget what it had been like to be an outcast. His cooperative gave shelter to countless people in need. He also knew, of course, that we were the best workers available. The women who were left alone belonged to the most cultured families. After all, it was the priests, teachers, civil servants, the intelligentsia who had been systematically liquidated. The wife of a fate-stricken priest or teacher worked harder than anybody else. On the one hand, she wanted to keep her job, and she did not want to worsen the situation of her children and possibly that of her husband (if the situation of our husbands could be worsened at all). On the other hand, she was reliable by virtue of her education. My closest colleagues were a priest deprived of his profession but not deported for some reason, and four political prisoners' wives. We worked for very little money, but we were happy to be allowed to work at all. . . .

Our cooperative, employing around five hundred people, operated successfully and kept growing. I worked there as a central cashier. All the workshops—the tailors, hatters, watchmakers, shoemakers, tile stove builders, flatiron manufacturers, and balance manufacturers—brought their daily income to me. I added up the money, entered it into the books, put it into bags, sealed the bags, and eventually handed them over to the bank couriers. The following day I received a certificate whether or not the money I sent corresponded to the account. I was in a much better situation than I used to be in my previous cashier's job: it was not my responsibility to take the money to the bank. I did not have to work overtime, unless the bank couriers were late, which meant an extra half hour at most. My work place was also close to our apartment.

It was customary that workers with a higher income rounded down the kopecks at the end of the amount of their wages. By the time I paid everybody's wages, the kopecks made up quite a nice sum; enough to buy some chocolate for the children. Nobody ever talked about this; it happened tacitly. Despite this bonus, paydays were the hardest for me. The employees of the cooperative, working all over the city, could not be gathered for meetings, so our boss held all the obligatory meetings on paydays. I was allowed to pay them only after the workers had sat through the meeting.

It was also my job to compare work sheets with reality. I did not see what went on in the workshops, but I knew that, for example, the tailors made and sold as many as three dresses with one work sheet; that was the only way for them to have some extra income. No one knew better than I how much such extra income was needed! Those people also had to get along somehow! They would have torn me apart if I had thought otherwise. We held together, and as a consequence, we worked in a good atmosphere, despite our misery.

A Woman Earns Respect as a Metallurgical Engineer

Antonina Aleksandrovna Berezhnaia

One of the more revolutionary aspects of Soviet communism was that it promised to liberate men and women from the sexist shackles of bourgeois middle-class mentality. In large part, this was because "building socialism" required so much work that the Communist Party refused to bar someone's advance solely on the grounds of gender. Consequently, many Soviet women became engineers, doctors, and government officials at a time when very few women in the West could attain such positions.

Antonina Aleksandrovna Berezhnaia was the chief refractory engineer for the steel mills in the Central Urals region. In this selection, she is interviewed by Anastasia Posadskaya-Vanderbeck about her experiences as a woman engineer in the 1950s, 1960s, and 1970s. The interview reveals that, although she was met with hostility by some of the men who reported to her, she succeeded in her position because she had the support of her superiors, all of whom were men. It also shows how high-level decisions within a state-run industry were made.

Antonina Aleksandrovna Berezhnaia, interviewed by Anastasia Posadskaya-Vanderbeck, "Overcoming an 'Incorrect' Birth," in *A Revolution of Their Own: Voices of Women in Soviet History*, edited by Barbara Alpern Engel and Anastasia Posadskaya-Vanderbeck, translated by Sona Hoisington. Boulder, CO: Westview Press, 1998.

Anastasia Posadskaya-Vanderbeck: Please tell me about your childhood.

Antonina Aleksandrovna Berezhnaia: My father's name was Aleksandr Ivanovich Berezhnoi. He was a very intelligent, hardworking Ukrainian. He himself worked a great deal and kept his estate in model order. But after the revolution, see, he worked as an agronomist on a *sovkhoz* [state farm]. They invited him to work there because he was a big specialist, despite the fact that he had been a landowner. But he was killed there as the result of an accident. He worked there for five years and then was killed. We were left alone. Things had come to the point that, well, as a matter of fact, children with such a past had nowhere to go.

Early Education and Training

How many of you were there?

There were three of us. Three sisters.

And your mama, was she still alive?

Mama was alive. But Mama managed to get us into a *detskii dom* [children's home] on the basis of a recommendation by the board of this sovkhoz where Papa had worked. We were in this detskii dom for five years. I studied in a model experimental school there and was a member of the Komsomol [Young Communist League]. Well, and then, see, it turned out that I couldn't get into a university because of my social origin. And so I went to work in a factory in 1930, the Tula arms plant. I worked there for two years, then started working two machines instead of one, and was considered a "shock worker" at the plant. And when they had the first conference of shock workers*—they weren't called Stakhanovites then, but shock workers—fifteen people were sent from the arms plant, and I was one of those fifteen. See, I was at that first conference of shock workers. I have such memories of it; even today I remember it!

What year was that?

* Shock workers were laborers who consistently exceeded their daily production quotas. Conferences of shock workers were periodically convened for the purpose of disseminating the methods of the most advanced workers.

That was in '31. At that time, I was . . . I was born in 1910, so that means I was twenty-one. But I worked unstintingly, of course. . . . And I was a member of the town soviet, they elected me. That was the beginning of my work as an activist. Well, and then I got married and went to the Urals. And in the Urals things were also very complicated for me: I had a family, but all the same I entered an institute of higher education, and in '40 I graduated from UPI, the Urals Polytechnic Institute, with a specialization in refractory materials.

So by that time it was possible for you to get into such an institute, right?

Yes, yes.

So your social origin was no longer an obstacle?

No, see, here's how I got in: When I was still in Tula at the arms plant, I was given recommendations by the party and union organizations, since I was a big social activist (she laughs). So that's how I got in. Well, and when I graduated from UPI here in the Urals, I went to work at the Verkhneselskii metallurgical works as a forewoman. I worked there for two years as a forewoman, and then, see, it was wartime. Conditions were very difficult at the works. We didn't even have dishes. Young people today haven't the faintest idea what things were like, then. We had to use metal cans for dishes. It was very hard, but the people really supported each other; they got along well. We worked twelve- or fourteen-hour shifts—not only at the factory, we even helped in the hospital, everywhere. That's how it was. But then I was promoted, and they made me head of this refractory shop. I worked in that capacity for three years. Well, how should I put it, production was my life, pure and simple. I really loved the factory, and I really loved my coworkers. We worked together very well. Things were hard, people would come and work fourteen hours, they would be hungry, but they had to go on working. I would go through the shop, and I used to sing them the song, "All Our Life Is a Struggle." They already knew that if our life was a struggle [she laughs], it meant we had to keep on working. They would run up to me and say: "Antonina Aleksandrovna, don't worry, we'll stay, we'll work another three hours."

Was this during the war?

That's right. It was during the war.

Were they women, for the most part?

Women and men. But there were fewer men, a lot of women. It's very hard to produce refractory materials.

Antonina Takes Charge of Five Factories

You know, they make steel in open-hearth furnaces, they pour it into molds. Steel is used everywhere—rails, everything is made out of steel. And in order to make the steel pour—it's a very hot metal—you have to add a certain element so that it adheres, so that this steel flows like a stream along this, along these refractory materials and doesn't get contaminated. And in this way it solidifies into clean ingots. And it was these refractory materials that we made. But there at the factory, besides my work in production, I had . . . I was a member of the party. And I carried out agitational work, I worked with the people, I ran study groups—all that in addition to my work in production. And then they recommended to the administration of ferrous metallurgy that I be made chief refractory engineer. And when I transferred into the administration, it was the beginning of very important work. They introduced me to the managers of the factories of whom I was supposed to be in charge. You can just imagine: At the first meeting called by the head of the administration, all these guys gathered, big, important, seasoned. And suddenly, see, the head of the administration said: "I'd like to introduce your new chief refractory engineer. I ask you to love, favor, and help her. She will be in charge of you." Five factories, understand? And these were big and important factories. And I was from the shop floor, from the shop floor; on the other hand, I knew production well. But all the same, this was something completely different!

I was then forty-eight. Of course, I already had a great deal of experience. Well, so the meeting ended. The men said good-bye to me coldly and went their separate ways. I went to the head of the administration and said: "You know what, send me back to the factory floor. I don't fit in here" [she laughs]. He laughed and said: "No, Antonina Aleksandrovna, I know you well, and you'll do fine in this work. We'll back you up. First, study each factory carefully, study everything; that way you'll figure out what you need to do." In addition, the Institute of Refractory Materials right here in Sverdlovsk was also affiliated with us, and this was an important organization, a research institute. Well, and so I began to work. I had a hard time, and my husband would say to me: "Just why do you need all this? Go back to the factory floor and take it easy." I said: "No. If I start something, I carry through with it to the end. That's the way I am." Period. Well, I began to go around to the factories. I went to one factory—I'll never forget it—the manager there, a big specialist, said: "Antonina Aleksandrovna, I'll give you the chief engineer, I'll give you the head of production, and they'll show you everything." I said: "You don't need to tear people away from their work. I know production. True, your factory is enormous, you supply the entire Urals with refractory materials, but I'll simply walk around and have a look at what is going on." And so I stayed there two weeks. And I did the same thing at each factory.

Getting Her Factories to Innovate

What exactly was your task?

As the chief refractory engineer, I had to know what sort of technology and equipment each factory had, the quality of its output, and its prospects. These were precisely the things that lay in my domain.

And did you write reports?

Yes.

One for each factory?

I'll tell you about that later. First, I made a careful study of everything. Well, three months passed. Then I said to the head of the administration, "Well, it's time to get down to work." I drew up a plan of development for each factory. I'll tell you later what it consisted of. When I arrived at one of the factories, they assembled a lot of people for a meeting. Up to this point, when they had production meetings, I was very unobtrusive. Sometimes I asked questions, sometimes I listened—I always wrote down everything, studied everything—but I didn't express any opinions, didn't introduce any proposals of my own. But at this meeting, see, I heard them out, and then I talked about each shop, I showed them what was wrong with their technology, where their equipment was outdated, where the quality was poor and why, and drew up a plan of development. They were amazed, see. When I laid out everything to them at the meeting, they realized that I had exposed their hands, that they couldn't hide anything from me, because I had talked with the workers, with the foremen. Everything had become clear to me. And what they needed to do was to introduce a rotary furnace. Then the factory manager got up and said: "This is all very good, but we can't do it. Just who is going to give us the money?" I said: "You have to do it. Otherwise the metallurgical plants will keep expanding, and you won't be able to supply them with refractory materials." That's the way it was at that factory and at a second factory and at all these factories. And when I arrived at the administration, I found that the head had been replaced and there was a new one. He was a big specialist but a very rigid and tough man. After he had looked at my plans, he said: "You mustn't forget that we can't give refractory materials top priority; that goes to metallurgy." I said that this was clear to me, because metallurgists always consider refractory materials secondary. But when the metal is of poor quality because of the refractory materials, then they always put all the blame on the refractory engineers. So, I said, the impasse had to be broken, the money had to be allocated. "But we can't allocate the money." Well, okay, I thought; my situation was very difficult. But I worked well with the others in administration. The head of the planning division, the head of the financial division, and the head of industrial and mechanical services all supported me, understand. They understood that I really wanted to accomplish something. And so the head of the planning division said: "Don't worry. The only thing you have to do is get the documentation for the project through the Institute of Refractory Materials, and the rest, the money, I'll give you." "But how?" "At the expense of construction funds. A great deal of money is allocated for open-hearth furnaces, but they don't use it all, they turn it around very slowly, money is left over, and I will give that to you." Well, then it was my turn: I went to the Institute of Refractory Materials, to the director there. He and I discussed the matter, but he was very indecisive: "Well, you know, this will take half a year; all of this will take a long time." I said, "No, we need to get this done quickly." I flew off to Leningrad. In Leningrad there was also an Institute of Refractory Materials, and in that institute was a remarkable specialist, the chief engineer of the institute, and he helped me. He said: "Okay, we'll draw up an agreement. Will you pay overtime?" "We will," I answered. And within three months they had prepared all the documentation. When they had completed all the documentation, the money was immediately transferred to the factory, and within two months they began construction. And after all this had begun, then the factory managers began to treat me quite differently, totally differently! And they would send a car for me and make polite requests: "Come, do come, even if it's just for a few hours. Look things over, check to see how things are going." That's how it was, and then the work went very well. But the work was very difficult, important, but also interesting, and I was very satisfied with it. Sometimes I think it was so difficult because here I was a woman in the midst of men, understand. Here you had to prove your ability to work, your knowledge, and only then did you earn their respect. Otherwise, they would have dismissed me completely.

Other Women in Industry

Were there other women who were also specialists like you?

Well, there were women in the institute, but they did research. But, see, here's another reason why I had a connection with the institute: I invented many things. For example, one of my inventions was displayed at an agricultural exhibit: I proposed a device that didn't exist in the Soviet Union at that time for the pouring of metal. It was new technology. I really liked all this. I didn't do it for money; at that time, money didn't interest me. We had money, they paid us well, we lived well. But the chief satisfaction was that you had accomplished something and it worked. That's what was really interesting! Well, they did propose that I get an advanced degree at the institute. But I thought, I'm no longer young; do I really need to do this? I'll end my days in production. So I didn't go for the advanced degree. That's how it was.

Antonina Aleksandrovna, did they offer you yet another promotion, perhaps to a higher position in administration?

Look, I had . . . my position was a very important one, because I was the chief refractory engineer in the entire Ural region, understand!? In my field, see, you couldn't go any higher. Well, what could they offer me at the institute? Since I didn't have an advanced scientific degree, they couldn't put me in charge of a laboratory. Then, too, that sort of work, which was more sedentary, didn't interest me very much. If I had gone to the institute in the first place, of course I would have written a dissertation. But I preferred production.

You said that in industry during the war the majority of workers were women. What about after the war?

After the war, men began to fill the ranks, they came back from the front. So there were more men. And in the refractory works we already had a lot of men because there was a great deal of technical equipment in these factories. What's more, there were these new furnaces, mechanized furnaces, which women couldn't operate. Rotary furnaces for the firing of brick.

But during the war didn't women do heavy work like that?

Yes, they did heavy work. Very heavy work, especially in the refractory shop. But all the work was manual. It wasn't mechanized because they didn't have the equipment. There was nowhere to get it. And then there were factories that had been evacuated to the Urals from the south. They were set up in the open air, and they worked in the open, too. I'll tell you, people really worked!

And did women who had been evacuated do factory work?

Yes, they also did factory work. We had a lot of women from Ukraine. They worked in the foundry, in the open-hearth furnace. But just the same, they always did heavy work, because they weren't skilled. They couldn't be given lighter work.

Most likely there were also educated women?

Yes, yes. Educated women as well. A lot of them.

Antonina Confronts a Bully

Antonina Aleksandrovna, look, in your life you had to work a lot with men, right?

Right. I'll tell you what was interesting about working with men in administration. It used to be like this: We'd have a meeting, a briefing session, and there would be eighteen of us, and I'd be the only woman! And in addition, I was the chair of the local union committee. And the head of the administration was very businesslike and knowledgeable, but he was really a tough guy and crude, crude.

Did he swear?

He didn't swear at the briefing sessions, but he loved to put people down. And we had one blast-furnace operator, he wasn't bad at the job, he was okay, but he was such a modest person. And the head of administration never called him by his name or by his patronymic. Just what did he call him . . . ? Aha, "Hey you, stand up, tell us, what's up in your shop?" But I, as chair of the local trade union committee, later, after everybody had left, I went up to him and said: "Why do you treat people like that, why? Don't you know how to treat people decently? Look, he's highly trained, he knows his work well. What gives you the right to humiliate a person like that?" I said: "You know what, cut it out. If you keep doing this, your behavior will be discussed in the local [union] committee." And he said: "Are you trying to teach me something?" I said: "I was elected by the people, and I have the right to criticize you, because this doesn't become you, it's simply a bad example for the whole group." He and I had run-ins, big ones. Well, all the same, work is work. And at meetings he would always look for a reason to discredit me, to see if somewhere in my sphere something had gone wrong, either project documentation was lacking or somewhere a factory hadn't met its deadline. But I didn't get flustered; I always gave him a good rebuff. And then, too, I had a lot of support from others in administration.

And, you know, what's also important, what's surprising is this: People weren't greedy for money, and that's surprising because in a material sense they didn't live very well, but nobody strove to earn money by dishonest means. Somehow things went along smoothly, people respected each other and were honorable when it came to their work. Everything was okay.

An Exile Struggles to Support Herself

Nadezhda Mandelstam

Nadezhda Mandelstam is the widow of Osip Mandelstam, one of the Soviet Union's most famous poets. She is also a poet in her own right. In 1933 her husband wrote a sixteen-line satirical poem about Josef Stalin; he was immediately arrested and imprisoned, and Nadezhda was exiled from Moscow. This selection from her memoirs describes the difficulty with which a "stopiatnitsa," a female exile, supported herself. Her experience was typical for many "criminals without crimes," the relatives of political prisoners.

During my wanderings I have met all kinds of ordinary folk and I have almost always got on better with them than with those who consider themselves the cream of the Soviet intelligentsia—not that they were so anxious for my company either.

Immediately after M.'s arrest I lived for a time in Strunino, a small cotton-mill town beyond Zagorsk. I had learned about it by chance as I was returning to Moscow from Rostov-the-Great, where I had originally wanted to settle. On the first day there I had met Efros, who went pale when I told him about M.'s arrest—he had just spent many months in the Lubianka [an infamous prison for political dissidents] himself. He was almost the only person during the Yezhov terror to get away with nothing more than expulsion from Moscow. When M. had heard, a few weeks before his own

Nadezhda Mandelstam, *Hope Against Hope: A Memoir*, translated by Max Hayward. New York: Modern Library, 1999.

arrest, that Efros was out and had gone to live in Rostov, he was staggered and said: "It should be renamed Efros-the-Great." I readily believed him when he advised me not to settle in Rostov: "There are too many of us here already." In the train on the way back I got talking with an elderly woman and when I told her I was looking for a room she advised me to get out in Strunino and gave me the name and address of some good people there—the man of the house, she said, didn't drink or swear. Then she added: "And the woman's mother has been in jail, so she'll be sorry for you." The people one met in trains like this were always kinder than those in Moscow, and they always guessed what my troubles were—even though it was now spring and I had sold my leather jacket.

Living in Strunino

Strunino is on the Yaroslavl railroad along which prisoners are taken to Siberia, and I had the mad thought that one day I might catch a glimpse of M. as he went past in the prison transport, so I got out there and went to the address which had been given me. I quickly got on good terms with the people and told them exactly why I needed a place to live in the "hundred-and-five kilometer zone" [political exiles were forbidden to live within 100 kilometers of Moscow]—though they knew without my having to tell them. They let me have a porch which was not in use, but when it got colder later in the year, they insisted I move inside with them—they screened off a corner of their living room with cupboards and blankets to give me some privacy.

I never hid the fact that I am Jewish, and I must say that among the ordinary people I have yet to encounter any anti-Semitism. In working-class families and among collective farmers I was always treated as one of them, without the least hint of what one found in the universities after the war—and now too, for that matter. It is always among the semi-educated that fascism, chauvinism and hatred for the intelligentsia most easily take root. Anti-intellectual feelings are a greater threat than crude anti-Semitism as such, and they are rampant in all the overstaffed institutions where people are furiously defending their right to their ignorance. We gave them a Stalinist education and they have Stalinist diplomas. They naturally want to hang on to what they feel entitled to—where would they go otherwise?

I made day trips to Moscow from Strunino to hand in parcels for M., and my meager resources—I had to sell off M.'s books—soon gave out. My hosts saw that I had nothing to eat, and they shared their tiuria and murtsovka [country dishes] with me. They referred to radishes as "Stalin's lard." They made me drink fresh milk to keep my strength up—though they had little to spare, because they had to sell a good deal of what their cow gave to buy hay for it. In return I used to bring them wild berries from the woods. I spent most of my day in the woods and I always used to slow down as I came back to the house in the evening: I kept thinking that M. might have been let out of prison and one of these days would come out to meet me. It is hard to believe that someone can be taken away from you and simply be destroyed—the mind can take in the bare fact, but it is still impossible to believe.

Working in a Textile Mill

That autumn I came completely to the end of my means and I had to think of work. My host worked in the local textile factory, and his wife's family were also textile workers. They were very upset at the thought of my taking on this drudgery, but there was nothing else for it, and when a notice about hiring new hands appeared on the factory gate, I got a job in the spinning shop. I worked on the spinning machines—each woman worker had to look after twelve of them. I sometimes volunteered for the unpopular night shift so that I could go to Moscow during the day to hand in a parcel for M. and try to get the information about him which no one would give me. Working on the night shift and running between one machine and another in the enormous shop, I kept myself awake by muttering M.'s verse to myself. I had to commit everything to memory in case all my papers were taken away from me, or the various people I had given copies to took fright and burned them in a moment of panic—that had been done more than once by the best and most devoted friends of literature. My memory was thus an additional safeguard—indeed, it was indispensable to me in my difficult task. I thus spent my eight hours of night work not only spinning yarn but also memorizing verse.

To rest from the machines the women took refuge in the washroom, which was a sort of club for us. They would stop talking and look vacant whenever some Komsomol [Young Communist League] girl intent on making a career came running in briskly. "Be careful of *her*," they would warn me. But when the coast was clear they let themselves go, giving me a picture of how their present life compared with the old days: "It was a long day then, but we kept breaking off for a drink of tea—you know how many machines we each had to work on then?" It was talking with them that I first became aware of how genuinely popular Yesenin is.* They were always mentioning his name and he is a real legend among the ordinary people: they felt he was one of them and loved him for it.

In the morning, once they were out of the factory gates, they stood in line at the store to buy bread or cloth. Before the war, material for making dresses was very hard to get, there was never enough bread and living standards in general were extremely low. People have now forgotten what it was like, and my Stalinist neighbors in Pskov were always insisting that before the war they didn't know what poverty was and that they had only learned the taste of it nowadays. It is remarkable how willfully oblivious of the past people can be.

In Strunino I learned that a woman forced to live beyond the hundred-kilometer limit was popularly known as a "hundred-and-fiver" (stopiatnitsa). The word reminded them of the martyred St. Paraskeva, and when I later told it to

* Sergey A. Yesenin was a poet who wrote anti-Soviet verse. He committed suicide in 1925 and wrote his last poem in his own blood.

[Russian poet Anna] Akhmatova, she used it in a poem. All the workers in the factory referred to me in this way, and they were all very kind to me—particularly the older men. Sometimes they would come into the spinning shop and offer me an apple or a piece of pie ("Eat some of this, my wife baked it yesterday"). In the factory cafeteria during the meal break they always kept a place for me and made me take some soup to "keep my strength up." Everywhere I found this warm sympathy which was shown to me as a stopiatnitsa. There was never the slightest hint of anti-intellectual prejudice among these people.

Discovered by the Secret Police

Once during a night shift two dapper young men came into the spinning shop, switched off my machines and asked me to follow them into the personnel section. This was located in another building and we had to go through several shops to get to it. Seeing us go by, other workers switched off their machines and began to follow us. As we went down some stairs leading outside, I was afraid to look around because I sensed that this was a way of saying goodbye to me—the workers knew only too well that people were often taken straight from the personnel section to the secret police.

My conversation with the two young men was quite ludicrous. They asked me why I was doing a job for which I was not qualified, and I replied that I had no qualification of any kind. And why had I come to live in Strunino? I told them I had no other place to live. "Why does an educated woman like you want to work in a factory?" At that time I still had no college diploma and was only educated in the sense that I had been to a grammar school before the Revolution and belonged to the intelligentsia—as the two men realized instinctively. "Why didn't you try to get work in a school?" "Because I don't have a diploma." To which one of them said: "There's something funny about this—tell us the truth." I couldn't make out what they wanted, but that night they decided to let me go—perhaps because of the workers who had gathered outside in the yard. They asked me whether I was working the night shift again the next day and told me to come back to the personnel section before I started work. I even had to sign a paper saying I would.

I didn't go back to the shop that night, but went straight home. My hosts were still awake—somebody had come to tell them that I had been hauled off "to personnel." The man produced a small bottle of vodka and poured out three glasses: "Let's have a drink and think what to do."

When the night shift ended, workers kept coming up to the house and stood talking to us by the window. Some said I should go away at once, and put money on the window sill for me. My landlady packed my things, and her husband and two neighbors took me to the station and put me on one of the early-morning trains. In this way I escaped a new disaster, thanks to these people who had still not learned to be indifferent. Even if the personnel section had not originally intended to hand me over to the police, I am certain they would never have let me go free after seeing how the workers had gathered to say goodbye.

Chapter 2

Making a Home

Chapter Preface

Two of the greatest challenges faced by Soviet citizens were finding a place to live and getting enough food to eat. Throughout its existence, the Soviet government struggled to address these basic problems of living without ever being able to solve them.

The rapid industrialization of the Soviet economy during the Stalin years required that whole new cities be constructed in the middle of nowhere, close to mineral resources and hydroelectric power. Priority was always given to building factories and other industrial complexes before housing, so many workers and their families were forced to live for months in tents and makeshift shanties. Once the construction crews got around to building apartments, the shortage of building materials resulted in living quarters that were small and shabbily built. The influx of factory workers into established cities such as Moscow and Leningrad put unbearable strains on local housing, but builders of new housing in the old cities operated under the same constraints as did builders in the new cities.

After Stalin, more resources were devoted to new housing, but the continued shortage of materials resulted in housing units that were more like barracks than apartments. Many families considered themselves lucky if their living quarters consisted of more than one room, and most urban apartment dwellers shared kitchen and bathroom facilities with everyone else on their floor. In short, most urban Soviets lived for most of their lives in dormitory conditions.

As new cities arose and old cities got larger, providing their residents with food became a major problem. Many of the peasants who had raised food in the pre-Soviet era had left their farms to become factory workers, so there were fewer workers to raise food. Making productive operations out of the collective and state farms took many years; in fact, they never produced the amount of food that state planners projected. The Soviet transportation system was woefully inadequate for shipping perishables from the farm to the many cities dotting the vast expanses of one of the world's largest nations, and much food simply rotted or spoiled en route.

As a result, Soviet citizens spent much of their time looking for food. Supermarkets, known as grocery pavilions, were usually understocked, and shopping at them was a tortuous process that involved standing in one line to get a rationing coupon, in a second line to pay for the item, and in a third to obtain the item. Perishables could usually be obtained without rationing at the collective markets in the countryside, but this necessitated spending an entire day traveling by rail to and from the market. Most Soviets became quite adept at buying whatever was available at the pavilion or the market, then bartering with their neighbors for the items they really needed.

Living in a Workers' Commune

Mary Mackler Leder

During the early decades of Soviet communism, industrial workers lived in housing that was assigned to them by their factories. Some living arrangements amounted to little more than a cot in a factory dormitory and meals in the factory cafeteria. Luckier workers, usually those who belonged to a Communist-sponsored group, were assigned space in a communal apartment building, where they could at least get away from the factory.

Mary Mackler Leder was born and raised in the United States. In 1931, at age fifteen, she moved with her Ukrainian-born Bolshevik parents to a small town in eastern Siberia. Later that year she moved to Moscow, where an aunt and uncle lived, to make a new life for herself. In this selection from her memoirs, she describes the workers' commune to which she was assigned by the Komsomol (Young Communist League), a Party-sponsored group for teenagers and young adults. The living arrangements depicted herein were typical of workers' communes in the 1930s and even in later decades.

The very next day [after being assigned to the commune], I set out for the Dinamo (pronounced Dee-NA-mo) Factory. It was located in the working-class outskirts of Moscow, the Proletarsky district, and it was one of a group of pre-Soviet factories that included the Moscow Automobile Association Plant (AMO) and a ball-bearing plant (Sharikopodshipnik). Dinamo, formerly owned by Westinghouse but nationalized and given a new name during World War I, manufactured electric motors for trolley cars.

My step-uncle accompanied me. We boarded a trolley car on Chistiye Prudi, not far from his apartment building, and it took us all the way to the factory, a forty-five-minute ride. After making sure that I was in the right place and that I knew my way back, he went home. I gave my name to the guard at the gate and he gave me a pass to the personnel department. I found my way by showing the pass to people I met and having them point in the right direction. I was asked to wait at the front desk in the personnel section. A few minutes later, a man walked in, held out his hand, and said in English: "My name is Paul Lifshitz. I am an engineer here and I have been delegated by the Party Committee to look after the needs of the foreign workers at the plant. Welcome!"

He had a strong accent which at the time I could not place. It was German.

Paul took me into the personnel director's office and interpreted for us. He helped me fill out the forms (which were minimal), accompanied me to the office where ration cards were issued, and warned me to be very careful not to lose them, as they would not be replaced. Then he took me to the Komsomol committee where I got my housing order.

A few days later, my step-uncle called a taxicab and I left his home, with my baggage. He went upstairs with me when we arrived at my new address. Apparently, it didn't really matter any more if it became known that I had relatives in Moscow.

The Commune

Tyufelev Lane number sixteen was one of a group of five-story apartment buildings about a ten-minute walk from the factory. The building was owned by Dinamo; the other buildings in the complex belonged to AMO. A three-room (plus kitchen) apartment on the third floor had been allocated to the Dinamo Komsomol committee to be used as it saw fit.

The brick building of three- and four-room apartments was typical of the housing constructed in the early 1930s. All rooms opened onto a central vestibule so that each room could be occupied by a separate family. There was central heating, electricity, indoor plumbing, but no bath or gas stove and no hot water. This was a great improvement on the one- and two-story wooden houses with wood-burning Dutch stoves for heating the barracks in which the majority of the factory workers lived.

I rang the bell. The door was opened by a fat girl with wavy, black shoulder-length hair, dark brown eyes, and a welcoming smile. She invited us in and introduced herself as "Valya." She took our coats and hung them up in the vestibule and showed us into a small room that contained four narrow iron beds neatly covered with white piqué bedspreads, four night tables with one top drawer and a storage compartment underneath, four chairs, and an oak wardrobe against one wall. She indicated the bed that was to be mine (farthest from the window, nearest to the door) and suggested that I put my suitcase under it for the time being. There was space in the wardrobe for my clothes. Outer clothing was to be hung on hooks in the vestibule.

Seven narrow iron beds lined the walls of the slightly larger room she took us into next. The beds were made in the same way as in the smaller room: white piqué bedspreads with a fold down the middle. Next to each bed was a night table. There was a large oak wardrobe at one end of the room and a square table with chairs in the middle.

Two youths sitting at the table looked up from their books and smiled. This was the boys' room, but it also served as the commune's dining room and social area. Both rooms were neat and looked clean. There was a loud-speaker attached to the wall in the larger room. These megaphone-shaped speakers were everywhere—in the hotel in Birobidzhan, in my step-uncle's and the Atlases' apartments, and in public places. They were outlets for the state central broadcasting system, a relay system that served as radio for the general public.

The commune occupied these two rooms. The third room of the apartment—the largest—was occupied by a young Party official and his wife who were there supposedly to keep an eye on the communards and help them out. But by the time I arrived, the official had been promoted out of the factory and was not in the least interested in his young neighbors.

The kitchen contained two work tables, one for the commune, the other for the couple in the other room. A Primus stove and two kerosene stoves stood on each table. The toilet was at the end of a hall between the kitchen and the vestibule onto which each of the three rooms opened. But there was no bathroom or washroom, and the small kitchen sink had just one cold-water faucet. Every inch of space in the vestibule was occupied by trunks, large wicker chests, boxes, and bundles. Each resident was assigned a specific amount of floor and wall space. Naked bulbs hung from the ceilings. . . .

The Residents

All the communards gathered for supper that evening. (I was to discover that this was unusual, as they worked different shifts and had different days off. There were no set mealtimes.) Valya had told me a little about them. All were skilled workers in the tool-making trades, some very highly skilled, though none was more than nineteen or twenty years old. Valya, in fact, was the oldest at twenty-one. She and Zina worked in the factory tool shop as lathe operators *(tokars)*. Shura, Vanya, and Yura had been *besprizorny;* that is, they had been among the millions of children made homeless in the aftermath of revolution and civil war. Large numbers of these "wild" children roamed the country, sleeping wherever they could and living by their wits. As in Nikolai Ekk's classic film, *Road to Life*, which appeared in 1931 (and was shown widely in the United States), these boys had been picked off the streets and sent to "colonies," actually reform schools for juvenile delinquents, where they had received an education and vocational training. Now they had gone to work at the Dinamo factory and to live in the commune. Shura and Vanya, one dark, one fair, were steady peasant types of few words, yet they were quietly friendly. Yura was bright-faced and full of curiosity. He was the only one who had attempted to impress his individuality on his "corner" of the room by placing a small picture of a landscape over his bed and a vase on his night table. The Levitin brothers, Boris and Yefim, worked in the factory and planned to go on to college. They were acquiring proletarian status so as not to be rejected when they applied. It was whispered that their parents were *lishentsi*—that is, persons deprived of their civil rights because of "bourgeois class origin." They spent little time in the apartment and generally kept to themselves. There was also an absent communard whose bed was being kept unoccupied for him. This was Volodya, who had gone to work as a volunteer at Magnitogorsk, a major construction project of the First Five-Year Plan, and was due back in a few months.

The seventh bed was occupied by an outsider, Haitin. (He was always addressed by his surname.) He had been expelled from the commune for disruptive behavior, the nature of which I was never able to ascertain. He did not share in the commune's expenses and had a special arrangement with Vassiona [the domestic] for her services. Haitin was employed at AMO as an electrician. Attempts had been made to evict him, but in vain. Eviction was a complicated process involving the factory administration and the trade union, as well as the district housing authorities, and he had succeeded in blocking the process with the help of AMO organizations. Haitin was tall, broad-shouldered, with straight black hair, black eyes set close together, and a habitual expression of amusement on his face. He seemed older than his nineteen years. He spoke Yiddish fluently.

This was my first experience in dormitory living. I had never gone to camp as a child and, except when cousins visited us, had never shared a room with anyone but my younger sister (and a very large room that was, with walk-in closets!). However, by now I knew what crowded conditions people lived in and I accepted my lot without a murmur. I had no choice.

Living by the Communist Principle

The commune had been established three or four years earlier, one of several Komsomol communes in the Proletarsky district. It represented a vanguard attempt to live by the communist principle: From each according to his ability, to each according to his needs. Members turned over their earnings and ration cards to a common treasury. Ration cards were " attached" to specific shops where some unrationed food and other necessities were also available. Some of the commune's money was set aside for housekeeping, Vassiona's salary, and other regular expenses. Each communard received pocket money for transportation, for the very inexpensive meals at the factory canteen, for "culture" (entertainment, books, sporting goods), and for small extras.

Our commune was not a voluntary organization in the sense that a group of congenial people decided to live together. Applications for membership were submitted to the district Komsomol committee with a recommendation from the applicant's place of work, in this case, the Dinamo factory. The applicant had to have a good work record and had to be active in Komsomol affairs. For young people from out of town who had no place to live, a communal residence was preferable to a cot in a factory dormitory, where they would often share a room with ten or fifteen others in a wooden barrack with no basic conveniences. Given housing conditions in Moscow, I was considered lucky to have been admitted to the commune. It was the intervention of the Komsomol Central Committee that did it.

Many of the members of the Dinamo commune had been living in it from its inception, though there had been some turnover. The first chairman had left. He had made the young girl who was their domestic at the time pregnant and the factory finally gave the young couple a room of their own somewhere else. He used to visit us once in a while, never with his wife. No one had been chosen to succeed him as chairman. Vassiona, whom I came to detest for her vulgarity, filthiness, and sly, troublemaking ways, made all the decisions regarding meals and practical matters, sometimes consulting with one or another of the communards. Meetings to discuss other matters were called by anyone who wished to take the initiative. . . .

Major items of clothing, such as. . . shoes, suits, coats, and household goods were usually purchased by order. If an order was given to the commune, the members decided at a meeting to whom it should go and allotted money for the purchase. If it was given to an individual communard, the commune paid for the article. Orders were usually issued by the factory trade union committee or administration, sometimes to individuals for good work, but more often for communes and collectives to distribute. . . .

Mealtimes

Breakfast was standard: tea, bread and butter, or more often margarine, hard cheese or sausage if the ration had not been used up, leftovers from the day before. The person on duty for the week rose before the others in the morning, lit the kerosene or the Primus stove, and put the kettle on for tea. We had one meal at the factory. For those working the morning shift, this was the noon meal; for those on the night shift or swing shift, it was the evening meal. The meal in the factory canteen was the main meal of the day. Dinamo was a heavy industry enterprise and therefore in the highest supply category. Meat was served several times a week. What was for dinner at the factory was a daily topic of conversation among those coming from and going to work. Communards in the evening shift had a meal at home, usually around three o'clock. The morning-shift people came home shortly after four, but were frequently detained by meetings or classes, so that until late in the evening there was usually someone eating supper at the table in the bigger room. Often, there were several of us at the supper table, talking, laughing, and joking.

Vassiona was not expected to serve us. Someone, usually

the person on duty if he or she was not at work, heated a large pot of whatever soup Vassiona had made that day, stuck a ladle into the pot, and set it down in the middle of the table. We helped ourselves to the food. What we ate depended on what Vassiona had managed to procure that day in the store or at the open market. At the so-called "collective farm market," peasants stood at long wooden tables with little piles of this and that, mostly vegetables (cabbage, sometimes onions, carrots, potatoes) and dairy products. Money was not important. Barter was the prevalent means of exchange. We all had "worker" category rations, so there was more than enough bread and sufficient cooking oil in supply. Vassiona exchanged bread, cooking oil, sugar, and soap for milk, butter, pot cheese, and whatever else we needed that was available. Frequently, the soup was cabbage soup, with or without pieces of meat in it. Potatoes fried in sunflower seed oil were standard fare. Millet porridge was often served with meat or eaten with milk. For dessert, there was a kind of pudding called *kisel*, made with potato starch and milk or, later in the year, cranberries or red currants.

Frequently, no one was at home when I returned from work. That hour or so when I was alone was precious to me. I could shut the kitchen door, heat water in the kettle or in a big pot, and wash myself at the sink. In the morning, I hardly had time to splash cold water on my face and hands, grab something to eat, and run. But in the afternoon, I could read, write letters, or write in my diary. I could sit still in an empty room.

An empty room! A room of my own, where I could close the door and shut out the world—I was obsessed by this dream. It was a fantasy I dreamed of nearly all the years I lived in the Soviet Union. (By the time I finally got a room of my own, it hardly mattered anymore.)

Cleanliness and Hygiene

Valya, Zina, and I managed to keep our room tolerably clean, no thanks to Vassiona. Vassiona willingly picked up after the boys, dusting and washing the floor in their room, but she did ours only when we made a fuss. Females could do their own cleaning. She seldom bathed or changed her clothes. Our room was stuffy, but I could not persuade the others to keep a window . . . open. The double windows were sealed for the winter. It was too cold, they said. Besides, the night air was bad for you.

I remember how my first day at the commune, I woke up in the middle of the night. Something was biting me. I switched on the light. More bedbugs! The girls laughed at me the next morning (the light had not awakened them). "Fresh meat," they said. "You'll get used to them. Don't squash them, they'll stink up the room if you do."

I had no intention of getting used to them. I kept at Zina and Valya until they agreed to help me do something about the bugs, and they made Vassiona help, much against her will. We turned all four mattresses and poured boiling water into the springs. By repeating this procedure every once in a while, we managed to keep the bedbugs under control.

Not so the cockroaches. When I turned on the light in the kitchen late at night, swarms of black insects the size of large beetles scurried off in all directions. The first time I saw them, I quickly turned the light off, ran into the boys' room, and pulled Yura after me into the kitchen. "*Tarakany*," he said, and shrugged his shoulders.

My Russian-English dictionary told me the meaning of *tarakany*. I had never seen cockroaches this size. When I told Valya about the cockroaches, she showed me a packet of yellow powder called pyrethrum, kept on a kitchen shelf, and said it sometimes helped. I sprinkled it in all corners, but it did not do much good.

Not Cultured

My efforts to improve hygiene, especially in the "places of common usage"—to get everyone to flush the toilet after using, to do something about the roaches and bedbugs, to get them to open windows more often—were not taken seriously. I composed signs with the help of the dictionary, often using the wrong word to everyone's amusement, and tacked them up. No one corrected the signs and no one paid attention to their exhortations.

On the other hand, they found some of my habits not *kul'turno.* The Russian word *kul'turno* has a multitude of meanings, the least of which is "cultured." It may refer to, among other choices, hygiene, cleanliness, manners, erudition, or forms of recreation. Its emphasis changed over the years. In those days it was a potent word, expressing a goal toward which the Soviet people in general and the proletariat in particular were striving. *Nye kul'turno*—not cultured—conveyed strong disapproval. I did not use a fork to spear a slice of bread from the bread basket on the table, as they did. That was *nye kul'turno.* I'd forget myself and start whistling (though I was not very good at it). Whistling indoors was bad manners for males as well as females. ("You're not in the middle of a field!") I'd come in from the street and throw my coat down on the bed instead of hanging it up in the hall. This was shockingly *nye kul'turno.* (This last had a sound basis. You never knew what you might bring in on your collar from the factory cloakroom or a crowded streetcar. I got into the habit of inspecting my outer clothing carefully when I came in from outside and hanging it on a hook in the hall.)

Living in a Communal Apartment Building

Maya Plisetskaya

Housing was in critical shortage throughout the Soviet Union for its entire history. Part of this was due to the immense destruction wrought by World War II, and part due to the tremendous expansion of the Soviet economy. As a result, most families were crammed together into one or two small rooms in communal apartment buildings.

In this selection from her 2001 autobiography, Maya Plisetskaya, a world-renowned ballerina with the Bolshoi Ballet, describes the living conditions in the building where she lived for almost fifty years. As the passage indicates, this building bore more resemblance to a college dormitory than it did to a modern apartment complex.

And so I graduated from the ballet school in 1943, was accepted into the Bolshoi Theater, danced a few noticeable parts, and received my first award. I was given a room 10 meters square [about 1000 square feet or the size of a typical basement] in a communal apartment, in a building owned by the Bolshoi Theater at No. 8 Shchepkinsky Passage. The name Shchepkinsky is derived not from the word *shchepka* (wood chip) but from the name Shchepkin, a well-known nineteenth-century actor of the Maly Theater.

There are three theaters on Theater Square in the heart of

Moscow—the Bolshoi, the Maly, and the Central Children's Theater. I know of no other place in the world where there are three theaters located on a single city square. It used to be called Theater Square until it was renamed Sverdlov Square, a name that is just as ludicrous as the name Kirov Ballet. [Yakov Sverdlov was the first Soviet president, Sergei Kirov the Communist Party boss of Leningrad.]

The Apartment Building

My renowned apartment building was located on the other side of the famous quartet of horses drawing Apollo's chariot. At night after performances cumbersome, dusty, stinking stage props were brought in and out of this narrow passage with a crashing din that the quiet of the night amplified. Trucks rumbled. Armchairs, tables, trees and doors, walls, windows, staircases and vases, chandeliers, balconies, and sphinxes were hurled about, to the sound of colorful curses. This went on every night until about three or four in the morning. That's when I learned to manage without sleep!

My room was tucked away in a large, endless communal apartment, located on the second floor of the three-story building. (There was a construction office on the first floor, the second and third floors were set aside for performing artists. A theater dining hall is located there now). Seven doors opened out onto a long ugly hallway, but there were nine rooms. Twenty-two people lived in the apartment. A single toilet served all of them; they locked it with a simple nail bent into a hook. And there was a single kitchen in which humpbacked, roughly planked tables of varying heights were pushed together—each family had its own table. There were four gas burners, and you had to patiently wait your turn to cook soup or boil water in the kettle. There was also only one bathtub, used according to a strict schedule. Fortunately, the theater was just across the way, a minute-and-a-half walk from the house. Impatient tenants would run over to the Bolshoi to take a leak.

There were two rooms hidden behind the first door. The singer Borovskaya, a first-class coloratura soprano, lived there. She had a husband, a maid named Katya, and a Chekhovian lapdog named Umka. She vocalized in the morning, and the entire apartment knew her vocal exercises by heart.

The Residents

The Borovskys lived a rich life. They had St. Petersburg furniture, an antique chandelier with candelabras, stern portraits in thick frames of rich mahogany, and a card table with a light with an enormous red-lace shade hanging above it. To me this seemed the height of chic. Borovskaya used to sing in the Maryinsky Theater, then she was invited to Moscow. The government capital drew the best talents like a magnet. She sang Verdi's Gilda especially well, but her appearance, alas, had gone downhill; something about her reminded me of a dachshund.

Three of the Chelnokovs lived in the next room. God only knows how they wound up in the Bolshoi's building. The head of the family was a pilot who, at the end of the war, would fly to Berlin on bombing missions. My ballet girlfriends perceived the aura of a hero around him. His wife languished waiting for him, moaning and groaning, while his son Seryozhka drank—serenely, though a great deal.

Nina Cherkasskaya, a dancer in the corps de ballet, occupied the third room. All her physical qualities contradicted the idea of ballet—thick, crooked legs, a feeble body, a parrot's-beak nose—but she worked in the ballet theater her whole life. All sorts of things were possible in ballet in those days. Her husband, Vasya, also drank, and he, too, drank a lot. He loved to whisper complaints to the neighbors in the kitchen about the injustices of life after he'd had a few. He'd been through the war, but instead of gratitude he was being forced to work in a place that didn't suit him. When the mood struck him, he even hinted that he had refused to be a stool pigeon . . . Nina also had a pockmarked maid named Nyura and three sluggish, obese, neutered cats. They all slept in one room.

In the next room—the fourth one—lived Pyotr Andreyevich Gusev, a well-known ballet dancer, teacher, former director of our ballet school, and choreographer (at the end of his life he even acted the part of Marius Petipa in a film). Later he was also artistic director of the Bolshoi Ballet. I remember him kindly—he was the one who invited Vakhtang Chabukiani to choreograph *Laurencia.* (I also had some bright days. There is a film entitled *Masters of the Russian Ballet*, in which Gusev dances the part of Giray in *The Fountain of Bakhchisarai* and I dance Zarema.) His wife, Varya Volkova, danced in the corps de ballet and was beautiful but a little blind and deaf. She constantly asked everybody about everything in our dim kitchen, blackened by smoke from frying potatoes, thereby causing a lot of confusion in our collective life. A nanny would come over with her daughter to the Gusevs during the day to look after little redheaded Tanya Guseva. All her childrearing efforts also took place in the kitchen. The nanny taught Tanya good manners, scaring her away from her favorite place in the hallway, where she had gotten into the habit of sitting on her potty. Gusev himself used to make wisecracks and kept the kitchen rolling in laughter.

Next to them lived my aunt Mita and her husband, Boris Kuznetsov, professor and doctor of some technical science or other. He was reserved, taciturn, and blindingly handsome. Had he been born in Hollywood, he would have eclipsed Robert Taylor.

Fedotov, the dramatic tenor, and his family lived in the two corner rooms facing noisy Pyotrovka Street. He sang all the leading parts in classical operas and sang them well. But he was fat and paunchy, as is customary in the world of tenors even today. His wife was German and taught German in school. During the war she passed herself off as Estonian, since all Germans were sent to Siberia as a precaution. It wasn't difficult to do because their maid Alma actually was Estonian. Alma spoke Russian atrociously. She earnestly warned children inclined toward hygiene, "Without mama's question, you can't go bath, because one man went bath, he went bath and drownded." A saucepan to her

Addressing the Housing Shortage

Housing was always scarce in the Soviet Union. The Soviets inherited a housing shortage from the tsars, then made it worse by emphasizing the construction of factories and industrial complexes over dwelling places. World War II made a worse situation intolerable when millions of homes in thousands of cities and towns were destroyed. After the war, efforts to provide decent housing for Soviet citizens were thwarted by a growing population and rising expectations. Henry W. Morton, in a western review entitled Soviet Politics and Society in the 1970s, *addresses the Soviet Union's "capacity to sustain and endure continuing change." This excerpt discusses the persistence of the housing shortage despite a massive government effort to eliminate it.*

Soviet builders, on orders of their political leaders, have constructed more housing units in a decade and a half than any other country in the world. Between 1956 and 1970, 34.1 million units of housing were built, and 126.5 million people, more than half of the country's population, moved into them. . . . Why does housing still remain such a problem? . . . A rising expectation accounts for part of the problem. Almost all my Soviet acquaintances and those officials whom I interviewed in 1971 told me that they lived in separate *(otdelnie)* apartments, usually in new housing districts in the outlying sections of cities. Ten to 15 years ago most of them lived in one room, sharing a communal apartment with several families. Yet, many are still not satisfied with the amount of space they occupy. . . . They would like to upgrade their living conditions further; to acquire a separate room for themselves or for their children to sleep in (other than the living room); or, in cases where two or even three adult generations of a family live together (which is common), to receive a separate apartment for the parents or for the children, particularly if the latter have married.

Henry W. Morton, "What Have Soviet Leaders Done About the Housing Crisis?" in Henry W. Morton and Rudolf L. Tokes, eds., *Soviet Politics and Society in the 1970s.* New York: Free Press, 1974, pp. 163, 187.

was *yakobchena*, which meant *zakopchennaya* (blackened with smoke). Whereas we, mistaken ones, thought that the saucepan belonged to Yakobson, who was a frequent guest at the Gusevs'.

The Fedotovs' son Rudik inflicted great suffering. He was forcibly and agonizingly taught music. Every damned day for years he practiced the same piece, stumbling over the same passage. I could hear Rudik's piece so clearly through the thin, slightly listing wall, that I had the impression he was accompanying Borovskaya right in my room. But the worst misfortune befell us when his singing lessons began. He had no natural singing voice whatsoever. What the tenants heard was deafening, hysterical shrieking. Fortunately, this ordeal came to an end one day: Rudik became passionately interested in film. His multiple wives did not hang around long. They didn't fancy his voice either. But they frequently added their own noise to all the discordant sounds of our apartment. The majority of the tenants of No. 23 later moved to the first postwar cooperative theater house on Gorky Street. As fate would have it, in 1963 my husband and I bought Borovskaya's three-room cooperative apartment from her and still occupy it to this day. The conductor Kirill Kondrashin rented it before we purchased it.

One Telephone

The sound recording of our daily life would be incomplete in my narrative if all this were not permeated with the incessant, shrill ringing of the only telephone—a single phone for all of us!—which was screwed to the wall in the hallway. The people who called us had no sense of time. There were phone calls in the dead of night and in the earliest part of the morning. We were informed about the minutest details of each other's lives.

There were also guests who visited. Sometimes, rushing through the hallway, I would stumble upon the writers Leonov, Kataev, Vishnevsky, Kirsanov (the latter carried off two volumes of my collected works of Pushkin, which I regret to this day), the satirist Laskin, the violinist Madatov, film director Roman Karmen, the pianist Emil Gilels . . .

The neighbor's lively, resilient son drove back and forth, day and night, like one possessed, in the hallway on his homemade bicycle, often knocking down lingering tenants who were shuttling between the kitchen and their rooms. Pyotr Gusev, who loved his sleep, would dash out into the hallway from time to time and demand quiet in a tense, quavering voice. The boy was proud and responded to Gusev's outbursts with leaflets, which he slipped under the tenants' doors: "Petie's an old fart . . ."

I lived in this apartment until 1955, when I was given No. 24, conductor Fayer's two-room apartment, on the same staircase landing.

Shopping with Grandmother

Zoya Zarubina

Under Soviet communism, obtaining food was a major occupation for most families. Even relatively well-placed families had to spend a significant amount of time standing in lines at the poorly stocked state stores, oftentimes to buy what was available rather than what was needed. As a result, bartering became a national pastime as well as a way to procure the necessary items.

Zoya Zarubina was a Soviet intelligence officer during the Cold War. One of her major accomplishments was translating from English into Russian the blueprints for making an atomic bomb that the Soviets had obtained from spies. In this selection from her memoirs, she describes how her grandmother helped get the family through the 1930s, when famine plagued the entire nation, and how her grandmother taught Zarubina to barter and to shop in state-run stores.

"Once when I was very young, staying with my grandmother, Evdokia, my father came home from work one day, and I ran to him to tell him about a theater where there were lots of lights and singing. I told him how much I enjoyed it and that they gave me something to eat and drink. My father looked sternly at grandmother and said, 'Now look here, you don't mean to tell me that you took her to church and had her baptized?' Grandmother answered, 'I sure did!' He couldn't scold her in front of me, but he wasn't

Inez Cope Jeffery, *Inside Russia: The Life and Times of Zoya Zarubina*. Austin, TX: Eakin Press, 1999.

at all happy. Religion was not accepted by the Party, but Grandmother never accepted the Party. She would take me to services now and then and would talk to me about it without using the word God very much. But she would say, 'I am a believer because we have been believers in my family for a very long time.'

"Somewhere I read recently that before the Revolution, Russians all trusted in God and thought that paradise would come in 2,000 years. But later on their religion became Communism—having equality, sharing everything, living a wonderful and happy life. I had taken it all in along with my school and the activities I was involved in and all of the wonderful, positive people who were our leaders. I was impressed with the loyalty, patriotism, and desire to do good things. But along with all of this, we had fear. I would talk to my grandmother, and she gave me that feeling of belief. My stepfather and mother were always at work so we learned much of our attitude toward people and life from my grandmother. She lived with us until she died in 1936 when I was sixteen. She died of heart failure at the age of 56, but she looked very old to me. . . .

Shopping with Grandmother

"While grandmother was still with us she could help us manage with food. She had relatives in the country who had gardens and grew their own food. It was the time when rationing was very severe. She would go to the country and trade clothes for sacks of potatoes. When she had several sacks of potatoes, she would let us know by telegram that she was coming back on the train, and Leonid [Zarubina's stepfather] would meet her with a car. We would have roasted potatoes and sometimes potatoes in jackets, and we feasted for a while. There was very little meat or chicken, but we had a variety of cereals which grandmother would prepare in different ways by adding some pasta, or plums, or eggs to make it different.

"I was ashamed to go with Grandmother to the market. She would bargain and push and haggle over a few rubles or kopecks. I was embarrassed, but we would put everything together and be able to buy tissue, sugar, and things that were very limited in rationed goods.

"In the early thirties we started having what they called Torgsin shops. It meant trading with foreigners using foreign currency. You had to have gold to trade for the special coupons, but you could get unusual foods that were not on the rationing list. My grandmother sold the few little gold things that she had and got bonds for them. She wore a gold chain and cross which she never sold, but she gave up her wedding ring and other gold jewelry. Once in a while she would give the bonds to my mother and tell her to go buy whatever she wanted. We were very fortunate that we lived through it all because the times were very difficult.

"Once she wanted me to go do the shopping. It was very cold and my shoes were being mended and re-soled. Grandmother let me wear her boots, but they were white so she gave me galoshes to wear over them. It was so crowded in the tram, and I lost one of the galoshes. She really scolded me, and I was hurt. Later I realized that this was the one and only pair of galoshes she had possessed throughout her lifetime so we managed to get another pair of galoshes for her.

Practicing What Grandmother Had Taught

"Later in 1944 when my daughter Tanya was very small, she was learning to talk, but she took everything in that was happening around her. She was aware that we could only buy with rationing coupons, and she observed the bargaining. At the time I was going to the KGB specialized school of languages and got special worker's rations because I was an officer. I would collect loaves of bread for two weeks and take them to the market and exchange them for cream cheese, butter, soap, and vegetable oil. Tanya would go with my mother to shop, and one day she said, 'I know you bought me at the market! But what did you sell to get me?' Then she said, 'You are all impostors. I was not bought at the market—I was born but I still don't know how that happened!' No more single words and phrases for her. From then on she talked about everything."

Nearly Trampled to Death at the Grocery Pavilion

Nina Markovna

Food was always in short supply in the Soviet Union. As new industrial communities sprang up across the nation, the ability of central planners to supply these communities with the needed foodstuffs was severely strained. This situation existed partly because supply could not keep up with demand, and partly because the Soviet transportation system was simply not capable of delivering perishables over thousands of miles before they spoiled. As a result, Soviet shoppers bought whatever was available in the stores and were happy to have it.

Nina Markovna was born and raised in Dulovo, a small factory town in western Russia. In this selection from her memoirs, she recalls a trip she made to the local grocery store as a young girl in the 1930s. The poor availability of items and the time-consuming buying process she describes were typical in most places and at most times during the Soviet Union's existence.

The food that our cherished kitchen garden provided was of immeasurable help to us. In all Dulovo there were a couple of bakeries, a store where dairy products were sold, and a meat market. The shelves in all of them were empty most of the time since those stores were just not geared to provide enough food for the thousands of inhabitants of the area.

Nina Markovna, *Nina's Journey: A Memoir of Stalin's Russia and the Second World War*. Washington, DC: Regnery Gateway, 1989.

Grocery Pavilions

Dulovo also had two large grocery stores, pretentiously called "pavilions." One pavilion was located across from the factory, its revolving glass door spoke of modernity and progress. But it, too, could not sufficiently accommodate the populace, the store's door remaining most of the time unused. Still, the pavilion's glass display window was forever beckoning, promising, seducing one's eye with the chunks of hanging smoked hams, various types of sausages, carcasses of plump chickens, geese, and ducks; or with glistening loaves of bread, from black rye to white French loaves, and heaps of piled up *baranky* (bagels), some plain, some covered with poppy seeds.

And the vegetables! The fruit! What mouth-watering torment it was to stand by that glass store window, waiting for my parents to appear at the factory gate, and trying to persuade myself that those articles, those fairy tale articles, were just that—a fairy tale—all made of clay and porcelain.

The real items were seldom obtainable. On those rare days when trucks with food supplies arrived, the alert went out by word of mouth, spreading rapidly from one dwelling to another. Hundreds of foodseekers lined up for several blocks around the pavilion, praying silently, as my mother did, for something to be left when their turn came. Something! Anything! No one, with the exception of the very few who were first in line, expressed a preference for any specific item. Were it a chicken or a bunch of grapes, a pound of precious butter or eggs—all were gratefully accepted.

The second pavilion, located near our home, was a much smaller store than the one near the factory. Mostly bread and soy-based candy, dipped in artificial chocolate, were sold in this trailer-shaped pavilion. The candy lay in decorative piles in the store windows, sometimes for months, undisturbed, due to its mediocre taste and exorbitant price. Vodka, too, was occasionally dropped off in this store, together with wines and sweet liqueurs. From time to time the arrival of herring or cheese surprised the shoppers.

Because the store was near our home, Slava and I paid close attention to its activities. If merchandise arrived, we were to find the rubles left under the tablecloth for that particular purpose, grab a plate, pot, or shopping bag—since the stores did not provide anything in the way of packaging—and run to stand in line.

Trying to Buy Cottage Cheese

One late summer afternoon, while walking by the pavilion, I noticed a truck stopping at the store's back entrance, and ran to investigate. The saleswoman informed me that a shipment of cottage cheese had arrived. Delectable, not often seen cottage cheese! To spread it thick on a slice of bread, preferably white—black would do—to sprinkle some sugar on it—the best breakfast in the world! Being very perishable, it was available rarely, as were all items requiring refrigeration.

I was aflame, yet I had neither money nor the dish. I knew that in a matter of minutes the place would be buzzing with shoppers, and the cottage cheese would be gone.

"Auntie," I said to the sales clerk, "I am Nina, Mark Illarionovich's daughter. Please, auntie, reserve some cottage cheese for me. Be so kind."

"All right, kid. Four in the family? You'll get one kilo, one quarter per person."

Wow! Two pounds of that gorgeous stuff! I shot like a deer toward home, grabbed the dish, found the rubles, and with the same speed, approached the pavilion once more. Too late! People ran in droves toward the store, especially the ones who were on their way home from work. On top of that, it was pay day, when practically every man made it his duty to stop in the pavilion for a liter of vodka. He was not deeply interested in the arrival of cottage cheese, leaving it up to his wife to worry about such matters. But he was interested in his liter. Those men had to enter through the same door as the people who came to buy cheese. Tired, hungry, impatient for a relaxing drink, men were pushing, cursing, spitting, and smoking their ever-present coarse Russian tobacco—*mahorka.*

When I reached the line, I tried to sneak between the standing men, sort of torpedoing myself through the ocean of human bodies, moving steadily toward the store entrance.

Some men swore violently, others good-heartedly shouted, "Hey! You! *Glista!*" calling me the affectionate, but unappetizing nickname for a skinny child—a tapeworm. "Where do you think you're squeezing yourself to? Wait your turn! Aha! Aren't you Mark's little *glista?*" and they propelled me forward.

I finally reached the cheese counter, but I did not receive my purchase. Instead, I was given a ticket.

"There, girlie," the saleswoman pointed to the corner where a cashier sat. "Go pay the cashier. Come back to that counter, there. See?" and she pointed to still another clerk. "That girl will give you the cottage cheese." The procedure in all the stores of the Soviet Union was devised by the government in such a manner that a shopper had to stand not only once in line, not only twice, but three times in order to collect the purchased item.

I took the ticket given me, and started to squeeze toward the cashier. There was no breathing space between the shoppers, so that I could do nothing but follow the human flow, being hemmed in on all sides by the sweaty, *mahorka*-permeated men.

The cashier was not far from me any longer, when the manager barked out, "No more vodka! Finished!"

Trampled in the Attempt

The men began to curse, push women aside, and hurry to the exit door, not wanting to waste any more time in trying to find a fresh vodka supply. At one point I received such a jolt that the all-important numbered ticket and money I was holding, fell out of my grasp to the floor. Without those two things there would be no cottage cheese! I began to lower myself toward the floor to salvage the lost items when another wave of pushing men threw me completely off balance and under their stampeding feet. Heavy boots started to hit my shoulders, my buttocks, my head, pressing my face into the filth-covered floor. I wanted to scream, to let the stomping boots know that I, Nina, was under their feet! Yet, no air came to my throat to help me utter a sound. After several people kicked me, unconcerned about what it was that they were stumbling over, one man decided to inspect what was under his feet. I, by then, had become extremely weak, dazed by what was happening to me, my body growing numb.

"It's Mark's girl!" my savior shouted. "Fellows! What the hell are we doing? Killing Mark's little tapeworm!" He and a couple of his buddies lifted me up and prepared to carry me home.

"Cottage cheese," I managed to squeak out weakly. One of the men ran to the cashier, paid for my purchase, and brought it out triumphantly. "A present," he said, smiling.

Neither Slava nor my parents were home yet. The men placed me on the sun-warmed *zavalinka* [earthen wall built around a house to protect it from snow and mud] and with apologies, left to pursue their hunt for spirits.

That evening Mother bathed my body in hot, then ice-cold, water, massaging it with sunflower oil.

"Don't scream, little one," she commanded, "I must massage all that blue out and make the blood circulate."

She wrapped me later in a soft flannel sheet and tucked me into a mountainous down comforter. Then she brought me a glass of hot tea with home-brewed raspberry brandy in it, and sticking a thick lump of raw sugar between my teeth, said sternly, "No more pavilion shopping, girlie. Not on paydays!"

Chapter 3

Getting an Education

Chapter Preface

Soviet authorities placed a high priority on education, for several reasons. It was necessary to reeducate people socially and economically so they would participate willingly in the struggle to "build socialism." Huge numbers of engineers, technicians, and skilled laborers were needed to transform the Soviet Union from a backward, agrarian nation into a modern, industrialized one that could defend itself against the encroachments of the West. Education also served as the mechanism whereby future leaders could be identified and then trained to serve as the vanguard for the construction of a socialist society.

As part of its mission to proselytize youngsters, the Communist Party established the Young Pioneers. Modeled loosely on the Boy Scouts, the Young Pioneers offered boys and girls in middle school and high school the opportunity to participate in various social activities. At the same time, the youths were taught socialism and encouraged to exchange their bourgeois ideals for socialist ones. Many of the Young Pioneers' adult leaders were college-age students and workers who belonged to the Komsomol, or Young Communist League, a socialist version of the Explorers. Membership in both groups was voluntary and open to anyone who applied.

The Soviet system of higher education differed markedly from that of the West. College students paid very little for tuition and books, the bulk of these expenses being picked up by the government. Priority for admission was given to the children of blue-collar workers, the bright hope for the future of Soviet communism, while admission was generally denied to the children of "alien elements," members of the upper class as well as those people who had been accused of sabotaging, or "wrecking," the economic system.

A liberal arts curriculum, which trains students to be generalists by teaching them a little bit about many subjects, was virtually unknown. Most students took very few courses outside the core courses for their specialty, or major.

Vocational-technical training was held in much higher regard by the Soviets than in the United States. As with college education, vo-tech training was provided virtually free of charge. Another major difference between the Soviet and Western systems of vo-tech training was the Soviet emphasis on on-the-job training. It was not unusual for students to receive a month or two of classroom training, then be sent to work in a factory or shop, in many cases one that was being built from scratch, to learn how things were really done.

The Ideal College Student

Susan Jacoby

The Soviet system of higher education was quite different from that of the United States. Although only a few high school graduates were admitted to college, their tuition was heavily subsidized by the government. Unlike most U.S. college students, they did not study the "liberal arts," whereby students get an excellent general education by learning a little about a wide range of topics. Rather, they were enrolled in "specialist" curriculums that trained them to do a certain job but offered very few courses outside their area of concentration.

In the early 1970s, Susan Jacoby, an American education journalist, talked at length with a number of Soviet citizens while visiting Moscow. In this selection she summarizes her conversations with Tanya, a nineteen-year-old Russian college student who lives and attends school in Kazakhstan, one of the non-Russian republics in Central Asia. Tanya discusses how she got into college, what her courses are like, her extracurricular activities, and her hopes for the future.

If the Komsomol (Young Communist League) decided to hold a competition for the title of All-Soviet Ideal Student, Tanya would be a strong contender. She was what official propagandists would like to portray every Russian student as—earnest about her studies, dedicated to building Communism, generally serious in her approach to life. She loved sports and working on collective farms in the summer,

Susan Jacoby, *Moscow Conversations*. New York: Coward, McCann & Geoghegan, 1972.

disapproved of marijuana and admitted to only one secret vice—smoking ordinary cigarettes. Tanya contradicted the widely held foreign belief that most Soviet young people, especially students, are ideologically restive and deeply discontented with their society. She also bore out [the] conviction that many Soviet students have a distorted view of their country's past and, consequently, of the present. At the same time, she radiated innocent charm, gaiety and curiosity—all of which kept her from being insufferably pompous about her convictions.

An English Major from Kazakhstan

Tanya lived in Kustanai, a city of about 180,000 in the Soviet republic of Kazakhstan. We met for the first time when she was visiting relatives in Moscow during her summer vacation. In her letters and in long conversations during visits, Tanya gave me my most detailed picture of life in a provincial city, far from the superior physical amenities and intellectual ferment of Moscow. She was the only person outside of Moscow with whom I was able to establish a continuing relationship, and she saved me from the mistake of assuming that everyone in the Soviet Union thought and lived as my Moscow friends did.

At nineteen Tanya seemed younger than she was in every respect except her seriousness of purpose. Compared to most of the young people I met in Moscow, she was both socially and intellectually unsophisticated. . . .

On her trips to Moscow, she was thrilled at being able to buy *Moscow News*, a turgid English-language paper published by the Soviets that consists mainly of reprints from speeches by Party leaders. In Moscow it is read primarily by desperate American tourists who are foolish enough to come to the Soviet Union without an adequate supply of their own reading matter. But *Moscow News* was unavailable in Kustanai. Tanya, who was studying to become an English teacher, was delighted to practice her reading on some new material. . . .

Tanya's city in Kazakhstan had swelled in population during the past ten years as Russians emigrated—some lured by higher salaries and others by the promise of adventure—to help develop the Soviet "virgin lands." Her father was a construction engineer, one of a growing class of mobile military and civilian technocrats who are responsible for the physical development and administration of new projects ranging from dairies to dams. Like employees of large American corporations, the Soviet technocrats are on the move continually, from one far-flung province to another. They are usually Russian or Ukrainian, and they work in areas that are still educationally backward in comparison to the western part of the Soviet Union. In twelve years, Tanya's family had lived in five different towns. Her best friend, Irina, whose father was an army major, had moved to Kustanai from Tashkent, capital of the Central Asian republic of Uzbekistan. Before Tashkent, Irina's family had lived in a small settlement near the Arctic Circle. . . .

Tanya had chosen her teacher-training institute in Kustanai in order to remain near her family. On the basis of her academic performance, she could have been admitted to the larger and more prestigious University of Kazakhstan in Alma-Ata. In size and academic quality, the difference between the two is comparable to the gap between a small Midwestern teachers' college and a Big Ten university. "Alma-Ata is a city of over one million," Tanya explained. "I don't know how it would be, living there without my family. I have never been away from home for a long period of time. I really prefer to be surrounded by loving people." Her desire to stay at home was atypical, judging from the students I met both in Moscow and other cities. Most of them complained bitterly because it was nearly impossible for young unmarried men and women to obtain apartments of their own. The housing shortage is such that marriage is usually a requirement for receiving separate apartments from one's parents.

Getting into College

To enter her institute, Tanya was required to pass four examinations in Russian language, Russian literature, English, and Soviet history. There were seven applicants for every place in the foreign-language department and four for each place in the institute as a whole.

There are some eight hundred institutions of higher education in the Soviet Union known as VUZ (the initials stand for *vyshee uchebnoe zavedenie*, literally "institution of higher education"). Only about fifty of these are full-fledged universities with a wide variety of departments. The rest train students for jobs in specific fields such as teaching, engineering or medicine. Some are as prestigious as universities in their own academic fields. A foreign-language student, for example, would probably get a better education in his area of interest at the Moscow Institute of Foreign Languages than at Moscow State University, generally regarded as the best comprehensive university in the Soviet Union.

Competition for admission to universities is fierce; at the most prestigious in Moscow and Leningrad there may be fifteen or twenty applicants for every place. Only one out of seven high school graduates is now able to enter an institution of higher education; the proportion is expected to drop to one in ten by 1975. According to the 1970 Soviet Census, 5.5 percent of the adult population had some education beyond high school; 4.2 percent had completed their higher education.

Tanya was keenly aware that Soviet students constitute a privileged minority and at the same time defensive about any suggestion that they are a recognizable elite. "I realize I am fortunate to be a student," she said. "That is one reason I feel such an obligation to work diligently. But in our country, everyone has the right to a higher education, and it is free. In my opinion, that is one of the main advantages our system has over yours."

Tuition is free at Soviet universities and dormitory fees range from five to eight rubles a month. If a student eats in the college dining hall, food costs an extra ruble a day. Because she lived at home, Tanya's education cost her virtually nothing. . . .

Tanya was genuinely shocked when I told her that class

attendance is not compulsory at American universities. "If a student missed more than one class at my institute," she said, "he would be called before a meeting of the Komsomol and would receive a reprimand. If he continued to miss class, there would be much stronger discipline—he might be accompanied to class every day by a Komsomol member and required to spend his free Sunday preparing for class. A student who was absent regularly would not be allowed to remain at the institute."

Tanya attended classes five hours a day, Monday through Saturday. (The six-day week is standard both in universities and lower schools, although factories and offices have switched to a five-day week.) During her sophomore year, she spent three or four hours a day in English courses and one to two hours in a political course on the philosophy of Marxism-Leninism. All students are required to take political classes, but otherwise they are not allowed to take any classes outside their specialized field of study. A future English teacher does not take science; a future scientist does not study history or philosophy. There is no equivalent of the "basic college" courses that require most American university students to do some work in humanities, physical science and sociology. A Soviet student does not have any say in planning his own curriculum, other than the initial choice of a department. During the latter half of her sophomore year, Tanya's program was expanded to include the history of the English language and Kazakh.

Tanya and her Russian friends spoke Kazakh poorly or not at all, although most of them were likely to begin their teaching careers in Kazakhstan on a government assignment. All Soviet college graduates, with the exception of a few outstanding students who receive special "free diplomas," are required to spend two or three years wherever the state sends them. It is one way of meeting the need for trained personnel in rural areas where few people want to live or work, although most college graduates return to the cities as soon as their period of compulsory service ends. Kazakh-language schools exist, as do schools in nearly every language spoken by national minorities in the Soviet Union. (Yiddish is an exception, and this has fueled accusations that the Soviet government's policy is the suppression of Jewish culture.) But parents who want their children to get ahead in Soviet society generally send them to Russian-language schools. Tanya expected to teach in a high school, where she would have little need for Kazakh in her work. "It is a very difficult language," she told me, "and all of the high school students who are studying English will already speak Russian. Kazakh is my third language, so it would be much too difficult for me to teach English to students who did not speak Russian.". . .

The Curriculum

Soviet universities require an extraordinary amount of daily written work. They resemble secondary schools in this respect—a fact noted unfavorably by some prominent Soviet scientists who feel the universities do not give students enough scope for independent work and creative thinking.

Tanya said she spent three to five hours a day on English homework and one or two hours preparing for her course in the philosophy of Marxism-Leninism. "So, it is true, I spend between nine and thirteen hours every day either attending classes or getting ready for them. The work is difficult, but it is necessary."

Tanya also took on extra work beyond her course requirements. She listened intently to English-Polish records that were a present from a boyfriend stationed with the Red Army in Poland. Such records are widely available in Eastern Europe but are difficult to find in Soviet stores—especially outside of Moscow, Leningrad and Kiev. Tanya said the models of English pronunciation on the records had been extremely helpful to her. "It didn't matter that I couldn't understand Polish. What mattered was the speakers on the records were Englishmen, and I could see where I was going wrong in my pronunciation." The limited supply of English-Russian records sells out quickly in Moscow stores, but Tanya was able to find several and bring them back to

Kustanai. "All of my friends use them too," she said. "Everyone was very excited."

On the basis of Tanya's descriptions, I concluded that foreign-language teaching at her institute must be old-fashioned by Western standards. English lessons began every day with phonetic exercises based on some reading—usually a memorized proverb or poem. She gave me three examples of poems used in her lessons: Byron's "She Walks in Beauty," Longfellow's "The Slave's Dream," and Coleridge's "She Is Not Fair." After the phonetic exercises, students were required to retell several pages in their own words from the passages they had read at home. They made up short stories based on the new English expressions they had learned and either recited or handed them to the teacher in written form. I asked Tanya, "Do you ever try to have ordinary English conversation in class?" She replied, "That isn't part of the curriculum."

Tanya said the students often had to remain after class to copy portions of the text they were to study at home because "unfortunately, many of us have no textbooks." Irate letters about textbook shortages in the provinces appear frequently in Soviet newspapers. The complaints come from teachers, parents and students in widely scattered areas of the country. The less prestigious institutions in small cities like Kustanai receive short shrift when new books are distributed; sometimes texts do not arrive until weeks or months after the academic year has begun. The same problem occurs in elementary and secondary schools. Educators blame publishers, publishers blame truckers and the railroads and everyone blames the general shortage of paper in the Soviet Union.

Tanya's teacher-training institute was not even in the second rank of Soviet higher education establishments; it would be a mistake to conclude on the basis of her descriptions that foreign language teaching in all Soviet universities is equally out of date. . . .

However, Tanya's institute is probably more typical of the general level of instruction—particularly for future teachers. Most of the English teachers I met in ordinary Soviet

Practical Training for a Material World

Soviet education focused on giving students practical knowledge. The Soviet public school sought to give every child the skills required of a competent engineer, who was in tremendous demand in a rapidly industrializing society. Every child took four years of chemistry, five of physics, six of biology, and ten of arithmetic and mathematics. In addition, most boys and some girls were taught metal-working, carpentry, and small engine repair. Prospects for Soviet Society *provides a comprehensive overview of social change during the first fifty years of the Soviet Union's existence. This excerpt discusses Soviet educational philosophy and its implementation.*

The "golden thread" running through the entire Soviet effort at educational reconstruction since 1917, linking all periods together in common design, has been the attempt to make learning of practical value—to fashion the school as a gateway to the world of economic specialization and material production. . . . These principles came to be embodied in the system of "polytechnical education," or the "unified labor school." The quest for its implementation has never been fully realized, but as an aspiration it has influenced Soviet educational philosophy and programs from the beginning, and has recurred in various forms throughout the several periods of Soviet rule. The instruction of pupils through a series of steps linking scientific information with technical skills, followed by training in a vocational specialty, emerged from the early years of Soviet Marxist experimentation as the main format of Soviet polytechnical education. Scientific and technical theory, supported by general education in traditional academic subjects and accompanied by practical exercises and actual productive labor, became the central concern of Soviet educational development.

William K. Medlin, "Education," in Allen Kassof, ed., *Prospects for Soviet Society.* New York: Praeger, 1968, pp. 241–43.

high schools were as atrociously prepared to teach a foreign language as the average high school French or Spanish teacher in the United States. They had more excuse than Americans, of course, because their opportunities for foreign contacts and travel were severely limited. There are special language institutes and programs where the level of instruction is high, but they are geared toward students being trained for special jobs—usually in the Foreign Ministry or KGB. Tanya was a potential exception to the general mediocre run of high school English teachers, because she was so serious about trying to supplement her training. She displayed that earnestness during her acquaintance with me by constantly using her English in conversations, even though communication would have been easier in Russian.

She had only been studying English seriously for a year when I met her, but her pronunciation and vocabulary were both quite advanced. Her accomplishments contrasted with those of some high school English teachers I met who were unable to put together more than one sentence outside their classroom drills.

Extracurricular Activities

While Tanya's life beyond the classroom was placid and uneventful by Moscow standards, she did not seem to find it dull. Trips to Moscow were the high points of her vacations, but she enjoyed traveling almost anywhere in the Soviet Union. When I met her in August, she told me how sorry she was that she could not join her friends who were helping bring in the harvest on a collective farm. Soviet universities remain closed until October 1 so that students can help with the harvesting. "I had a stomach operation last winter," she said, "and the doctor said farm work was forbidden for a year. I had such a wonderful time when I worked on the farm last summer that I am very unhappy. We were paid 100 rubles, and there were students from all over. There were also lots of soldiers, and it was all very gay. I want to go again next year." Tanya's positive attitude toward compulsory summer work was not shared by the young Muscovites

I met; many of them tried fake excuses to free them from their duty to the state.

Tanya did not spend all of her time worrying about her English lessons and pining away for work on the *kolkhoz*. She was interested in boyfriends and ultimately in marriage, but like most young Soviet women, she could not imagine marriage and a family without a career. . . . Despite her romanticism, Tanya was determined not to marry until several years after graduation from the institute.

"I want to be free and independent for some time," she said. "After I finish school, I will go away to work somewhere in the country and be of service to my society. Then I will probably return to a city. I don't expect to get married until I'm sure of what I want in life. Children are a great responsibility, for one thing, and I don't want them until I am sure of myself." . . .

I asked Tanya what she did in her spare time. "As I only get 'good' and 'excellent' marks, I do have some extra time," she said. "Although I must admit it's not as often as I would like. I go to the movies, read English books, watch television or knit and crochet. I knit myself a scarf and am crocheting a white jacket for my mother's birthday. I love to dance too. But I don't know many boys who are good dancers." . . .

The books Tanya meant were, again, quite different from the literature that captivated young people in Moscow. Her favorite American author was—probably inevitably—Jack London. London is one of the few American authors widely available in translation in the Soviet Union. . . .

Of the classical Russian authors, Tanya preferred Mikhail Lermontov and Tolstoy. The Soviet authorities take a more positive view of Tolstoy than of any other classical Russian writer, mainly because he wrote about the harsh life of peasants. Dostoevsky was virtually banned during the Stalin years and is just beginning to be reintroduced in high school literature courses. The newest Soviet edition of *The Brothers Karamazov* is much shorter than the original because the censors have deleted most of the religious portions. . . .

Tanya was almost totally ignorant about the great writers and poets who were murdered or muzzled during the Stalin years and whose works have not yet been restored to their rightful place in Soviet literature. She had read virtually nothing by Osip Mandelstam, Boris Pasternak, Isaak Babel, Anna Akhmatova, Velimir Khlebnikov or Marina Tsvetayeva and in some cases did not even recognize their names. To draw a proper analogy, one would have to find an American university student specializing in foreign languages who had not read Yeats, Hemingway, Eliot, Auden or E.E. Cummings. . . .

Because she was interested both in music and in improving her English, Tanya listened regularly to the English-language broadcasts of the Voice of America.* I never met a student in any part of the Soviet Union who did not listen to the VOA. Although reception is hampered by jamming, Russians patiently persevere. For obvious reasons, English-language broadcasts are interfered with less than Russian-language ones. Many students also listened to the BBC, saying they preferred its news broadcasts because the reports were less slanted by American government propaganda. (I preferred the BBC for the same reason in Moscow.) The student consensus, however, was that the VOA offered better music than the BBC. Tanya loved jazz and rock records. "The classical music we can hear on our own [Soviet] records," she said. "But, to tell the truth, much of the music I like is on the foreign radio stations." . . .

An Accepting Attitude

Tanya's attitudes toward what she read in the official press were far less critical than those of anyone I knew in Moscow. It was instructive to learn this, because I had incorrectly concluded after six months in Moscow that no one believed anything he read in the official press. . . .

Tanya herself spouted an astonishing amount of historical misinformation, reflecting an uncritical acceptance of Soviet

* A radio station operated by the U.S. government; its powerful transmitters allowed its signal to reach most Soviet citizens.

textbooks. She said the U.S. Army never really saw hard fighting during the war because the Germans were so weak in the West that it was no chore at all to liberate France. President Truman had dropped the atomic bomb on Japan simply to frighten Russia with America's nuclear strength. . . .

Despite her belief in various historical iniquities of the West, Tanya was not suspicious of foreigners. She longed for an expansion of student exchanges and was regretful that so few foreigners lived in her town. The only ones she had seen in Kustanai were African students, whom she originally thought were black Americans because their clothes looked so expensive to her. "We like to meet people from other countries so much," she said. "I have dreamed of talking to Americans, to English people, to students from all over the world. We would argue about our differences, the way you and I do, but we would always be friendly. We all must live together on this earth and respect different ways of living and thinking."

Ridding Children of the Mentality of the Past

Lazar M. Kaganovich and Comrade Dorfman

To ensure that young people received the proper education and motivation to "build socialism," the Communist Party organized two youth groups. The Komsomol, or Young Communist League, proselytized among college-age students and young adults, while the Young Pioneers, which was modeled after the Boy Scouts (although it admitted girls and boys), was designed to appeal to pre-teens and teenagers. In the 1920s, the Young Pioneers were led loosely, usually by Komsomol members; the responsibility for planning and executing activities was given mostly to the children. By 1933, however, the adults had taken over, and the movement suffered from overleadership and formalism. These symptoms were the same ones the entire nation suffered from under Josef Stalin, who had assumed control in 1924. Under Stalin, expressions of initiative were often "rewarded" with banishment, imprisonment, or death.

In this selection from a 1933 Party investigation called "On Young Pioneer Work," Lazar M. Kaganovich, head of the Communist Party's regional organization in Moscow, interviews a Young Pioneer adult leader named Dorfman. A devoted communist, Kaganovich sincerely believed in the ideals of the Bolshevik Revolution, and here he is trying to find out how well the Young Pioneers are eliminating "all the

Lazar M. Kaganovich and Comrade Dorfman, "On Young Pioneer Work (Document 140)," in *Stalinism as a Way of Life: A Narrative in Documents*, edited by Lewis H. Siegelbaum and Andrei Sokolov. New Haven, CT: Yale University Press, 2000.

bad elements that have lingered from the past." Dorfman, on the other hand, is trying to avoid being punished for saying the wrong thing.

KAGANOVICH: What interests us the most is to hear from you what the Pioneers themselves are unhappy about; what kinds of opinions they express and what are they unhappy about?

DORFMAN: The major shortcoming is this. What does the Pioneer demand? That he be the master of his organization.

KAGANOVICH: Look at the kind of language you are using. We are not asking about this formula. Tell us in plain language, the way you talk with the youngsters and they talk with you.

DORFMAN: They are unhappy that there are no special technical groups.

KAGANOVICH: That's all they're lacking? That's all they miss?

DORFMAN: There's no color in their work.

KAGANOVICH: What does color mean?

DORFMAN: There's no club.

KAGANOVICH: Now you tell us, do they want to dance, and with whom? Do the boys want to dance with the girls, or don't they care?

DORFMAN: That of course makes no difference (laughter).

KAGANOVICH: Please, Comrade Pioneer leader, don't be shy, describe things in plain terms, don't try to use language that plays up to us. Tell us what Pioneers want. Do they want to have dancing, do they want to go to a museum, study art, or go to the theater or to the pictures? What do they want? Do they want to go to the pictures by themselves or to be taken, how many times do they want to go on their own, on their own without supervision, or under supervision? Do they want to be under supervision or not, and if so, how much?

DORFMAN: What do Pioneers want? They want to see a good picture. They don't like to go on an organized basis.

KAGANOVICH: Do they go on an organized basis?

DORFMAN: Yes.

KAGANOVICH: Are movies shown in school?

DORFMAN: Yes. Our school, for example, has a movie projector.

KAGANOVICH: What movies are shown?

DORFMAN: Most of all we run scientific pictures, as an aid, related to the study of some subject.

KAGANOVICH: But what pictures do the Pioneers like the most?

DORFMAN: Fights. Wherever there are fisticuffs, wherever people are leaping around.

KAGANOVICH: What else?

DORFMAN: Usually you can hear this kind of talk among the Pioneers: [cowboy actor] William Hart appears there. American actresses are in that. Now they'll spread the word, get about ten kids together and go to the pictures on their own.

KAGANOVICH: On what basis do they get together?

DORFMAN: The Pioneer unit has a work plan to go to the pictures three times a month. They fulfill that. But apart from that three or four youngsters get together and when classes are over they run to the movie theater to see a picture that interests them.

Dancing and Social Functions

KAGANOVICH: What pictures do the girls like the most? Or won't they say? What else do the kids want? Are they interested, for instance, in dancing?

DORFMAN: They're not very interested in dancing on a mass scale.

KAGANOVICH: Do they get to dance often?

DORFMAN: At every school dance.

KAGANOVICH: How many times a month are these dances held?

DORFMAN: Twice a month, but there are other evening functions as well.

KAGANOVICH: What functions are those?

DORFMAN: A shock worker's evening, a Pioneer detachment evening, and a school evening.

KAGANOVICH: Where are these functions held? Describe some specific function.

DORFMAN: Well we had an evening at school that was devoted to the issue of implementing the TsK's [executive board's] decision on the work of the Young Pioneer organization. This evening was arranged and conducted together with parents and the community. There was a short report at this function by the secretary of the party cell on implementation of the TsK's decision, then a representative of the TsK of the Komsomol spoke and afterward there was a brief report on the work of our Pioneer base. We awarded radios to the best shock working Pioneers as prizes. Five radios were handed out, and altogether twenty-eight people received prizes. After that there were amateur performances by the youngsters themselves.

KAGANOVICH: What kind of performances were these, and how did they manifest themselves?

DORFMAN: The units performed, they did physical-fitness exercises, they performed dances, there were individual dances, say from the ballet The Red Poppy and The Little Apple [a dance performed to a sailor's song of the same name—*Trans.*], and there was dancing for everybody. Then there was a stage production by the youngsters themselves and there was a living newspaper. And later, of course, there were refreshments for the youngsters.

KAGANOVICH: But does your school allow dancing in general? Where can the youngsters display some bravado and show off some tricks—is such dancing allowed? For example, the Kazachok ["The Cossack," a folk dance with an accelerating tempo—*Trans.*]? You don't have dances like that?

DORFMAN: The youngsters don't know the Kazachok, but they like to dance the russkaia ["The Russian," any of several Russian folk dances of varying tempos—*Trans.*]. They like "The Little Apple" and there are people who like to dance the Shamil' [named after the North Caucasian Muslim leader who defied Russian conquest in the mid-nineteenth century].

KAGANOVICH: And what about the foxtrot [a western

dance considered decadent in the Soviet Union] in your school? Do they dance it legally or illegally?

DORFMAN: They don't dance the foxtrot, and they don't dance it illegally, either.

KAGANOVICH: They probably dance it, you just don't know about it. Well, what else are the youngsters interested in? You referred to technical groups, what kind of groups are those?

DORFMAN: A radio group, a sawing group, and the cinema.

KAGANOVICH: What else?

DORFMAN: A percussion orchestra has been organized. They are very interested in this.

KAGANOVICH: Which children are most interested in these groups? Do these groups encompass a small group of children?

DORFMAN: The fifth and sixth groups. I would say that these groups do not encompass the majority, of course, and here is why—for one thing there are no leaders, for another there are no funds.

KAGANOVICH: What else are they interested in?

DORFMAN: They are interested in a lot of things.

Animosity

KAGANOVICH: And the children, the Pioneers, how do they get along with each other? Are they indifferent, or are there serious arguments, animosity, egotism, this kind of selfishness? What predominates the most? Maybe you could give a few examples from your work.

DORFMAN: I can describe an incident of a political nature and an incident of an academic nature. The first incident. This was the situation. One girl stopped coming to school. She was a girl from the second group—twelve years old. She didn't come in for three days, some old woman dragged her to church and she went around there with the priests, collecting money, cleaning windows, washing floors and so forth. I dealt with this matter myself. I went with two other Pioneers, we ascertained the reason, and we discovered that the well-known priest Vedensky and another priest twenty-two years old were exploiting this girl. We managed to find out where she lived. They were giving her packages to distribute, and what they were putting in the packages were prayers and crosses to distribute to adults.

KAGANOVICH: And you persecuted this girl in school, of course?

DORFMAN: On the contrary.

KAGANOVICH: Did she admit her errors? Did she write a declaration or not?

DORFMAN: We did not distribute wide notification of the detachment's meeting on this matter. We just had a preholiday rally. We just had a preholiday rally where we described this incident in passing. True, it was very easy for us to uncover this. The second incident has to do with how youngsters relate to other youngsters. We have situations like this one. A girl at our school is the chairman of the student committee *[uchkom]*, and based on the fact that she is the best student they began to persecute her: they started saying that she goes with somebody and that is how she gets good grades.

KAGANOVICH: How old is she?

DORFMAN: Fifteen, she is in the sixth group.

Fighting

KAGANOVICH: Are there fights between the boys, and if so, what causes them?

DORFMAN: Fights break out for no special reason. [Somebody says:] "Come out, let's fight." They just go for a fistfight to see who is stronger, who will beat whom.

KAGANOVICH: But in general, on what basis do fights occur, is there any hatred toward each other?

DORFMAN: Yes, there is.

KAGANOVICH: Based on what?

DORFMAN: We had an incident at school. A group got together—two boys and two girls. They got together at one boy's home on the pretext that they gathered to study subjects in which they were behind, and they shut themselves up in a separate room and took vodka in there. Their mother discovered these goings-on, she discovered that one boy came with half a bottle of vodka.

KAGANOVICH: How old is he?

DORFMAN: Thirteen. But they were not able to drink it, because the mother knocked, they opened the door and she found the vodka, took it away and gave them a real tongue-lashing. Somebody at school let the cat out of the bag, told a girl, the girl told the teacher, and they began to take up the issue in class. And after that they wanted to arrange a fist-fight. There are also fights that are related to thefts.

[BORIS] ROIZENMAN [a member of the party's Central Control Commission]: But are there any fights based on envy, say, somebody is doing better in his studies or eats better or dresses better? Do fights occur because of that?

DORFMAN: As an example, let's look at one class. We have boys who are well provided with money and pens and notebooks, they are fully provided for, yet they still steal, and not only in school, but from their own parents as well.

Is Progress Being Made?

KAGANOVICH: You don't seem to be able to describe relationships in general between the children, meaning their very essence.

DORFMAN: I did describe them.

KAGANOVICH: I am asking how much our children have already progressed in truly human terms with respect to how they relate to one another, with respect to getting rid of the mentality of the pest, egotism, vanity, selfishness, with respect to getting rid of all the bad elements that have lingered from the past. After all, we have to say that in regard to the human psyche 80 percent still survives from the past in our country. So I would like to find out how things are going with respect to ridding our children of these vestiges of the past.

DORFMAN: I have already cited this case. Because a girl is a good student, people try to take the wind out of her sails and begin to taunt her to the effect that she supposedly used to go with somebody or that she has a good relationship with the chairman of the uchkom and he is giving her good grades. Another situation has to do with thievery, when even well-to-do youngsters still steal. We have these cases too. Children sometimes assemble not only from a single building but from a neighboring one and organize attacks on children from other buildings.

KAGANOVICH: Are there ever any arguments at your meetings?

DORFMAN: Almost never. Somebody will give a report, people will ask questions, some people will have their say and at that point the meeting ends.

Learning to Run a Steel Mill

Nursultan Nazarbayev

Throughout its seventy-year history, the Soviet Union struggled to industrialize. Although it made unbelievable strides, it always felt an urgency to grow faster in order to keep up with the West, which had industrialized almost a hundred years earlier. As industry expanded, the need for engineers and trained personnel increased, and the educational system was hard-pressed to keep up with the demand. Consequently, on-the-job training became the norm for all branches of industry.

Nursultan Nazarbayev was the last prime minister of Kazakh S.S.R. and the first president of Kazakhstan after the fall of the Soviet Union. In this selection from his memoirs, he describes his early education as well as the on-the-job training program via which he learned to operate a steel mill. The selection indicates the obstacles to expansion faced by Soviet industry in the 1970s and the incredible hardships required of those who devoted themselves to building socialism.

School was not hard for me. When I started school, my parents did not yet have their own home. They were nomads who spent the summer in the mountains and the winter in the steppes, so I lived with my paternal uncle until I was in the fourth grade. He lived some way from the school, and I was awakened for school early in the morning by the roosters—there were no alarm clocks. Then I walked, half in my sleep, through the snow for six or seven kilometres. I

Nursultan Nazarbayev, *My Life, My Times, and the Future*, translated and edited by Peter Conradi. Northamptonshire, England: Pilkington Press, 1998.

would arrive at the school at about 5 or 6 A.M. If the guard was kind then he would let me into the school while he got the stove going. I could snatch some more sleep by lying next to it.

The only time left to do homework was at night because the tasks on the farm had to be finished first. I had to feed the cattle, clean the shed, fetch water and work in the garden. I learned to value time. I managed to get my homework done and even had an hour or so for reading. In those days, there was a huge difference between life in the cities and life in the countryside. Things that were accessible for boys in the city were often little more than a dream for us. We were much closer to the prose of everyday existence and the concerns of just putting some food on the tables which is why we had such modest demands for our future and had to be more realistic about evaluating our potential.

Although my mother and father could barely read, they had a great respect for people who were educated. My teachers were also insistent that I had the potential to go on to further studies. When I finished the compulsory seven-year education, the family was unanimous that I should continue studying. I had to go to Kaskelen, the nearest town, where there was a boarding school. It was not very far away, but it was the first time that I had lived away from my family.

To the Steel Mill in Temirtau

When I finished school, all attention in Kazakhstan was focused on a new city, Temirtau, where one of the Soviet Union's biggest steel plants was under construction. I saw an advertisement in a newspaper for the Temirtau Technical School which was accepting Young Communist League members to be trained for the plant. The course was for one year and all expenses were to be paid by the government. When I showed it to my father, he thought about it, then he sighed and said: 'Well, son, go ahead and see the world. If you have troubles, come back: this is your home.' Within a few days, I had gathered together the necessary papers and left.

Although I had my father's blessing to go to Temirtau, my

parents were not enthusiastic about the idea. Karaganda, and the surrounding area, including Temirtau, had a bad reputation because there was a well-known *Gulag*, a prison camp, there. There was also a local criminal gang which instilled terror among the residents.

My first impression of Temirtau was of a tiny town in the middle of an enormous construction site. There were cranes, trenches, foundations, pits, heaps of metal, sand, mounds of construction waste and tents—but no roads. When I arrived, the first blast furnace and electric power plants were being built.

We had just started to work when all of us with a secondary education were offered the chance to go for training at the steel plant in Dneprodzerzhinsk, in Ukraine. The Kazakh leadership, wanting to have enough trained local people for the Temirtau plant, had decided to send us to the Soviet Union's major steel centres to learn 'on the job' about the steel industry. Four hundred of us were sent off: some to the Urals, the rest of us to Ukraine.

On the Job Training in Dneprodzerzhinsk

The Dneprodzerzhinsk plant made a bad impression on many of the newcomers, including myself. Few of us had been raised in a city and we had only a vague idea about the conditions in which Soviet industrial workers had to live and work. It is understandable how a young man from the steppes reacts on seeing a steel plant for the first time. The noise is thunderous, sparks are everywhere, and all sorts of things fly through the air and threaten to fall on you. Molten cast iron runs like water in a canal and it is terrifying to go near it. The prospect of spending my whole life in that environment was depressing.

During the time we spent there, we used to scan the newspapers for reports on how work was proceeding at the plant in Temirtau. Would we finish our training in time to be the ones who started up the plant? Would we be capable of running such a large enterprise? I was recently looking through some old newspaper files and recalled the tense, and at the same time festive, atmosphere of those days. Journalists did not spare their superlatives in describing the heroic builders of the country's huge new steel plant. Just reading their reports made us feel enthusiastic and proud to be involved in this major national effort.

Suddenly, in August 1959, rumours began circulating around the factory of trouble in Temirtau. We heard that troops had been sent to the city, that there were casualties and that construction had been stopped. In those days of rigid state control of the media, the fact that the newspapers had nothing to say about the plant seemed to confirm the truth of the rumours, which became more detailed by the day. Then, one of the workers, who owned a radio, described how he had tuned in to Voice of America [radio broadcast] and heard President [Dwight D.] Eisenhower asking [First Secretary Nikita S.] Khrushchev, who was touring the United States at the time, about the reports of trouble. Although Khrushchev denied that anything had happened, we were now convinced.

Later, we found out what had happened. The young people who had gone to work in Temirtau had been becoming more and more unhappy with the living conditions there. Typically, for the Soviet system, the factory was being raised at lightning speed, while the workers themselves had to live in tents and hastily erected barracks. Often there were not enough protective outer garments to go around, supplies of food were terrible and the water was often contaminated. By the summer of 1959, many of the workers had simply had enough. So, on 29 July, a crowd of thousands of bricklayers, concrete layers and assemblers gathered on a square by the headquarters of the construction site to complain to the management. When they saw that no one was going to come out to talk to them, they took justice into their own hands, and started looting the grocery stores and consumer good shops. That night troops entered the city and shooting began. Even today, no one can say how many people were killed, although there were certainly tens of them. There were also some foreigners present: a group of Bulgarians who had been sent there by their country's Young Communist League. A curfew was declared and some people were arrested. Later, the 'ringleaders' were tried and punished. This, it should be remembered, was the period of the so-called Khrushchev 'thaw', a time when the then Soviet leader promised to build Communism on our planet within 20 years.

On the Job in Temirtau

By the time we returned to Temirtau, life had largely returned to normal. To our surprise the shops were especially well-stocked: the food stores had black and red caviar, sturgeon and good quality cognac and wine; the clothes shops were full of imported items—a rare luxury in those days. The reason was clear. After the unrest had been quelled, the authorities took urgent measures to 'pay off' the workers in order to prevent the same thing happening again. Such was the importance of the plant that even Leonid Brezhnev, the future Soviet leader, had gone on an emergency visit to Temirtau to see what had gone wrong.

On 2 July, 1960, the blast furnace finally went into operation. It was the only one of its kind in Kazakhstan or Central Asia. The day was marked by big parades, rallies and speeches, but the festivities were soon over, and the average life of the workers remained miserable. Our own living conditions were particularly intolerable: after a short time in damp and dirty basement accommodation, we were moved to an unheated dormitory where we kept warm by sleeping in twos on iron cots covered with mattresses. There was no place even to hang out our clothes to dry. We left our canvas work-clothes out in the frost because it was easier to put them on when they were frozen than when they were wet and heavy. There were no recreational facilities—the only entertainment that people had was big fights. Murders and other serious crimes were rife. We survived because we were young and strong.

The Training of a Communist Leader

Andrei Gromyko

In *What Is to Be Done?* (1902), Vladimir Lenin argued that revolution in Russia could only come about at the instigation of a cadre of trained professionals or, as he called it, "the vanguard of the proletariat." To this end, the Soviet Communist Party devoted much time and energy to identifying and grooming prospective leaders in the struggle to "build socialism" throughout the Soviet Union, even after the Bolshevik Revolution had been won. This effort included preferential treatment for loyal young Communists in the form of admission to the best schools and generous stipends to support them while they studied.

Andrei Gromyko was the Soviet Union's minister of foreign affairs (in essence, the secretary of state) from 1957 to 1985. In this selection from his memoirs, he outlines how he rose in the ranks of the Communist Party beginning at age thirteen. The selection demonstrates that, while loyalty to the Party was rewarded generously, Communists were expected to sublimate themselves to the Party's interests.

At the beginning of 1923 [at age thirteen], I was elected secretary [i.e., chairman] of the village cell of the Young Communist League, the Komsomol. Instructions affecting every aspect of village life were handed down to the local cells by the local Komsomol committee. The Komsomols were supposed to set an example to the peasants and

Andrei Gromyko, *Memoirs*, translated by Harold Shukman. New York: Doubleday, 1989.

the village intelligentsia, and we took this very seriously.

As I zealously read my instructions, I felt almost as if I was communing with Karl Marx himself. My family put up with my work, but at first did nothing more than that. However, when they saw other villages doing their best to get their own candidates put forward for election they took a more active interest.

In January 1924 Lenin died. It was a fierce winter. I remember struggling through great snowdrifts to get to school, where a funeral meeting had been arranged. Our teachers made speeches, reminding us how much Lenin had done for us and for all the workers and peasants of Russia.

The villagers talked of nothing but the death of Lenin. They asked: 'What will happen now? How are we going to live without Lenin?'

They thought that as Komsomol secretary I ought to be able to tell them. What could I tell them, when I was hoping someone would tell *me?* Then I remembered something I'd heard: 'The revolution was carried out by Lenin and his helpers.' So I replied: 'Lenin has died, but his helpers, the party, still live. And we will live with it.'

After I had completed seven years of primary school and then trade school in Gomel, I went to the technical school in Borisov, not far from Minsk. I lived there in a one-storey wooden house that was famous because Napoleon had slept there at the time he was retreating from Russia with his bedraggled army. It was still called 'Napoleon's', with some irony at the expense of the bankrupt emperor.

A Card-Carrying Communist

I joined the Communist Party in 1931, while I was in Borisov. I had dreamed of doing so ever since I first began to understand the difference between a poor peasant and a landlord, a worker and a capitalist. I received my party card just before the meeting that elected new officials, and at that meeting I was immediately made secretary of my party cell.

I was thrilled by my work in the party. Just as before, as a Komsomol, I was working closely with other people, dealing with the problems of the day, always in the thick of things. Party members in those days—as indeed throughout the history of our state—were in the front line, in the most important and difficult jobs. Not only did we have to explain and agitate in favour of party policy, the main topic at that time being the collectivisation of agriculture, but we were also the first to give up our Saturdays or Sundays to do voluntary work, willingly going wherever we were sent, collecting firewood, unloading wagons, wherever another pair of hands was needed. The party and the Komsomol understood our difficulties and loyally sustained the fire of communist conviction in our young hearts. . . .

I studied for a further twelve years after leaving primary school: first trade school in Gomel, then technical school in Borisov, then the institute in Minsk and finally postgraduate studies in Minsk and Moscow.

I had decided that I wanted to study the social sciences, and was confirmed in this when, at the age of sixteen, I made up my mind to read [Friedrich] Engels's *Anti-Dühring*,[1] whatever the effort. The fact that I was already running political study circles and that I had been elected secretary of the Komsomol collective bolstered my intention. It sounds hard going now, but once I'd started I found I couldn't put the book down, so clear was Engels's exposition of Marx's ideas. I had first heard about Marx's *Kapital* when I joined the Komsomol. I realised it was his major work, and after some months of trying I eventually got hold of a copy. I discovered then what a difficult book it was and noted places that I would study further 'when I was cleverer'.

As I was already a communist, and had been party secretary at the technical school, I found myself being sent on frequent missions by the party authorities, sometimes as often as twice a month. From Borisov, and later from Minsk, I was sent to help in the collectivisation, the consolidation of the collective farms and the strengthening of party work

1. This book advanced the socialist theories of Karl Marx while attacking those of the German socialist Karl Eugen Dühring. It did much to promote Marxist thought.

in the villages. Sometimes I had to deal with agricultural procurements also.

After two years of study in Borisov I was appointed head of a secondary school not far from Minsk, in the district of Dzerzhinsk, where my wife was working as a veterinary technician on a state farm. Thereafter I was simultaneously teaching and running the school, and continuing my studies as an external student at the institute.

Sent by the Party to Graduate School

One day a Central Committee representative of the Belorussian Communist Party came to see me with an unusual offer.

'The suggestion is that you should move on to postgraduate work—if you're interested, of course.'

'But I haven't yet done all my exams at the institute,' I objected.

'Don't worry. Work for the exams, and then, after them, you can go straight into postgraduate work.'

I asked for some time to think it over.

What worried me was the financial aspect. By this time we [he and his wife, Lydia] had our first child, Anatoly, but as a headmaster I was getting a good salary and I was afraid a graduate stipend would lower my family's living standards.

I was sent to talk to the people in Minsk. Professor I.M. Borisevich, who headed the commission at the university there, announced at the end of our interview: 'In view of your educational, labour and social record, the commission proposes that you join the specialist postgraduate course which has just been established here in Minsk.'

I naturally asked, 'What sort of specialists are to be trained here?'

He said, 'We have in mind economists with a broad background, both applied and theoretical. The Institute of Red Professors in Moscow is training social science teachers for our high schools. The idea is to do something similar here, in our graduate school.'

I told the commission frankly that I had had enough of living on a student grant. Borisevich assured me that after a short time graduates were to be paid a stipend in line with the party maximum—in other words, a decent living wage.

'Once you've taken the institute exams, you'll have no hardship,' he went on. 'You're well known here and you'll be taken good care of. The postgraduate course doesn't start for another six months, which gives you plenty of time.' Then he added: 'Whether you accept the offer or not, I happen to know that they intend to transfer you to work in Minsk.'

As I would be leaving Dzerzhinsk in any case, I agreed to the postgraduate course, and in 1933 moved with my family to Minsk. At first we took a private apartment. The professor's prediction about the party maximum had been right, and it was quite adequate for us.

Then the serious work of the postgraduate course began, directed by Professor Borisevich and his assistant, Professor Klimko. I remember that poor Klimko had lost an arm in the civil war. The first six months of the course were devoted to political economy, philosophy and English, and the teaching staff were first class.

We were enrolled in the Belorussian Academy of Sciences and, not long after we had joined, when the Academy put on a reception for some anniversary, we postgraduates were invited together with leading scientists and distinguished academicians. We were amazed to find ourselves treated as equals and placed at their table to enjoy what was for us a sumptuous feast. We realised then that not for nothing did the Soviet state treat its scientists well: evidently science and those who worked in it were highly regarded by the state. I must confess in all honesty that it was after that meeting with the academicians, when I saw how well the state looked after its scholars, that I decided, if I was given the choice, I would enter academic life.

Transferred to Moscow

But then, in 1934, an incident occurred which was to affect the entire course of my life. We were told without warning that our group was to transfer to Moscow to a similar institute. We thought about it, and after a while we decided not to protest. As the saying runs: 'If you're a mushroom, into the basket you go.' So in March 1934 my little family, with all our worldly goods packed into three suitcases, moved to Moscow. I well remember my feelings on the journey. An inner voice told me that soon I really would be walking on the famous flagstones of the Kremlin and looking at its walls close up, instead of on a picture postcard.

We were to be housed in Alexeyevsky, a student settlement on the north-east edge of the city. The second Romanov tsar, Alexei Mikhailovich, had had his palace there, though by now all that was left of it was its name. Alexeyevsky was a real student town, with young men and women wherever one looked, and we lived there quite comfortably until we got a really good apartment from the Academy of Sciences in a new block on Chkalov Street, which we shared with a young virologist called Mikhail Petrovich Chumakov. He has since become a world authority on poliomyelitis.

The director of the Moscow institute was M.A. Lurye, an eminent economic theorist. My postgraduate work at the institute was scarcely different from what I had been doing in Minsk, while my party missions in the Moscow region were similar also: dekulakisation, strengthening the collective farms and explaining party policy and the international situation to workers in both town and village. I also had to keep a check on local progress with the party's literacy programme, and lecture on theory—for example, on Lenin's *Development of Capitalism in Russia.*

I recall during one such trip, when it came to fixing up my lodging for the night, the chairman of the local soviet gave me a choice: 'Either you can sleep in a hut where they have a lot of children, which might be noisy, or you can do what other officials have done, and sleep on the hay in a barn.' I remembered sleeping comfortably on hay as a boy, when I had taken the horses to their night pasturing, so I opted for the second choice.

The chairman took me to the barn. When we were in the

yard, he casually observed: 'Not so long ago, in another barn nearby, an official who'd been sent here was killed by enemies of the Soviet regime.'

In fact, the night passed without incident. Even so, I did not sleep as soundly as usual.

During my time at the Moscow institute I was lucky enough to attend meetings with some famous revolutionaries in the All-Union Society of Old Bolsheviks. The club had been founded while Lenin was still alive, and had been formally organised in the early 1930s as a place where veteran Bolsheviks could meet to talk over old times, as well as to discuss the current situation.

Only party members of at least eighteen years' standing could join, and by January 1934 the society numbered more than 2000. Its aim, according to its statute of 1931, was to draw on the revolutionary experience of the Old Bolsheviks to help the party educate the young and to collect historical material. Although the members quite often met among themselves, meetings for which we young communists were given tickets were infrequent events which we were very keen to attend. . . .

A Job as a Research Worker

In 1936, after three years of postgraduate study, which included further English-language classes and writing and defending my dissertation, I was given a job as a research assistant at the Academy of Sciences Institute of Economics, which was then headed by the academician M.A. Savelyev, an Old Bolshevik and comrade of Lenin.

I assumed that my position as a research worker was stable and permanent. I had a secondary job as a teacher of political economy at the Moscow Institute of Civil Engineering, where my students included several who became famous later. At that time teachers were frequently as young as their students, which was true in my own case, and I often felt awkward; I would have liked to look older than I was.

At the same time, I had a party job running a circle for the political and economic education of scientific workers at a large factory in Moscow. It consisted of about thirty people, and topics included foreign as well as domestic affairs. I was to learn later that the commission of the Central Committee which selected candidates for the diplomatic service took these classes into account when planning my career.

One day at the end of 1938, having been made scientific secretary of the Institute of Economics, I was summoned by the then president of the USSR Academy of Sciences, the botanist Vladimir Leontyevich Komarov. I was puzzled at being called by so eminent a scholar.

He announced: 'We want to make you scientific secretary of the Academy's branch in Vladivostok.'

I cannot say I found this an appealing offer, so I said, 'I'm still only a young research assistant. The job requires at least a doctor of science.' What I was actually thinking was: If the president of the Academy were a psychologist rather than a botanist he'd no doubt see through me and I'd be on my way to Vladivostok.

Luckily he agreed to leave things as they were, but urged me to reconsider.

From Economist to Diplomat

As events turned out, I was not destined to continue as a research worker. At the beginning of 1939 I was invited to a Central Committee commission that was selecting new personnel for diplomatic work. When I was called in I immediately recognised V.M. Molotov and G.M. Malenkov.[2]

I was told: 'You are being considered for transfer to work of a foreign policy nature, probably diplomatic.'

I am not sure even now why the commission picked me. No doubt the frequent trips I made to explain the party line on domestic and foreign policy played a part, and the fact that I was at the top of my postgraduate group in learning English may also have helped. When I was asked what I had read in English, I mentioned a few books and then added

2. Molotov was the Soviet Union's foreign minister from 1939 to 1949 and from 1953 to 1956. Malenkov was one of Stalin's chief lieutenants and served briefly as first secretary of the Communist Party after Stalin died.

one that had interested me: *Rich Land, Poor Land*, by the American economist Stuart Chase. Nothing more was said, though I felt I had the commission's approval.

A few days later I was summoned once more to the Central Committee, where they told me: 'You are to be transferred from the Academy of Sciences to the diplomatic service—if you agree.'

A short conversation ensued and I told them I accepted.

Chapter 4

Redefining Morality

Chapter Preface

In order to "build socialism," Soviet Communists realized that it was essential to wean their fellow citizens from the bourgeois ideals of the past. In addition to reeducating the populace concerning the evils of the old way of thinking, Soviet Communists attacked the institutions and belief systems that propped up such ideals. Meanwhile, they worked to undermine nonproductive practices such as excessive drinking and gender discrimination.

For centuries, the Russian Orthodox Church, a branch of Christianity more closely related to Roman Catholicism than to Protestantism, had reaffirmed the tsar's right to rule Russia with near-absolute power. In order to rid Russia of the tsar's influence, it was necessary to do more than simply execute him and his family. The church that upheld his authority also had to be destroyed. To this end, the Soviet government worked assiduously to drive Orthodoxy into extinction. Priests were harassed, beaten, jailed, imprisoned, and murdered. As a result, few of the faithful rose up to take their places, thus leaving congregations without spiritual leaders. Known lay church members were denied membership in the Communist Party, and their children were denied membership in the Young Pioneers and the Komsomol. Quite often, the faithful were also denied employment, housing, and food rationing coupons, thus making it virtually impossible for them to exist in Soviet society. Children were taught in school that religion was only for backward people, and were made to feel ashamed of their parents and grandparents who persisted in their faith. In time, religious suppression and persecution spread to those socialist republics where Catholics, Jews, and Muslims constituted a significant proportion of the population, with the same results. By the time of the Soviet Union's fall, very few people openly practiced a religion.

As religious fervor decreased, alcoholism increased. Men had always gotten drunk on vodka during the tsarist era, but a number of observers have remarked that drunkenness seemed to rise markedly under Soviet communism. Since drunkenness caused absenteeism and injuries at work, thus decreasing productivity, the authorities strove mightily to put an end to it, with little success.

The most prevalent nonreligious bourgeois ideal that Communists worked to eliminate was the "double standard," which discouraged women from working outside the home. The tremendous demand for brains and labor absolutely required that women be allowed to work at whatever occupations they demonstrated an ability to do. As a result, Soviet women were encouraged and trained to become doctors, lawyers, engineers, and government officials decades before Western women were encouraged to do the same.

Putting an End to Drunkenness

Aleksandr V. Vlasov

One of the thorniest societal problems faced by Soviet communism was drunkenness. The effort to build socialism required that people work longer and harder for less compensation, and one of the results was an appalling rise in the consumption of alcohol. State efforts to solve the problem by reducing the production of vodka and other intoxicants were more than offset by the rise of bootlegging and moonshining.

Aleksandr V. Vlasov was the Soviet minister of internal affairs from 1986 to 1988; his closest U.S. counterpart would be the director of the Federal Bureau of Investigation. This selection is taken from a 1987 interview between Vlasov and an unidentified reporter with *Izvestia*, the official newspaper of the Soviet government. Vlasov acknowledges that alcohol abuse is worst in those communities that are undergoing the rapid transformation from an agrarian to an industrial economy. He admits that the problem will not be solved until people's private lives become more comfortable.

Correspondent: Aleksandr Vladimirovich, may I first ask what worries you particularly about alcohol-related crime today?

Vlasov: First of all I will say that more than one third of all crimes are directly linked to drunkenness. This amounts to one in five accidents or traffic accidents and one in nine fires; when it comes to crimes in the home, 60–70 per cent

Aleksandr V. Vlasov, "Alcohol as Solace and Barter," in *Social and Economic Rights in the Soviet Bloc: A Documentary Review Seventy Years After the Bolshevik Revolution*, edited by George R. Urban. New Brunswick, NJ: Transaction Books, 1988.

of them are the result of alcohol consumption. It is there—into flats, homes, and hostels—that drunkenness has crept from the streets and enterprises. This is its last firm bastion, which, unfortunately, is not being attacked with sufficient skill and energy. It is there that we find the rowdy drunk, the secret family drinker, the alcohol speculator, and the profligate who organizes binges with fellow drinkers.

I would like to talk frankly about the terrible danger of unrefined vodka and about the bootlegging which has recently come to light. Moonshining today—not only in the villages but in the cities too—has become a very dangerous refuge for alcoholism, is helping to turn people into drunks, and is a source of mercenary gain. It has a particularly strong hold in daily life.

Moonshining

Correspondent: Could you now explain about "unrefined vodka"—how widespread it is, how it is made, and so on?

Vlasov: I will try. Whereas in the recent past moonshining was typically a rural "criminal phenomenon," nowadays approximately 40 per cent of its "manifestations" are recorded in the cities. Along with alcohol speculators, bootleggers have begun to cause serious problems in urban residential areas and hostels. Geographically, the picture looks like this: moonshining is most prevalent in the RSFSR [the Russan Republic], particularly in large industrial centres in the Urals and Siberia where formerly there were no serious "hotbeds" of this sort. The RSFSR accounts for 72 per cent of all uncovered cases of moonshining, almost half of them in the Bashkir ASSR, Udmurt ASSR, Tatar ASSR, Altay and Krasnoyarsk krays, and Irkutsk, Kemerovo, Tyumen, Orenburg, Perm, Sverdlovsk, and Chelyabinsk oblasts.* The "moonshine disease" is spreading in the Ukraine, Belorussia, Kazakhstan, Lithuania, and Moldavia.

Who are our modern moonshiners? According to our in-

* ASSRs, krays, and oblasts were Soviet governmental subdivisions that correspond roughly to U.S. states and counties.

formation, 50 per cent are workers and employees of urban and rural enterprises; 15 per cent are collective farm workers. 61 per cent of all moonshiners are women (it is deplorable that wives and mothers are drawn into the pernicious process of poisoning their relatives by turning them into drunks!) I must point out that both the producers and the consumers of moonshine have grown younger: 52 per cent of those sentenced are below the age of 30, and only 20 per cent are pensioners [retirees]. Amongst those who had criminal charges brought against them last year, about 10,000 were people with higher or secondary specialized education, including 4,700 Communists and Komsomol members. . . .

Correspondent: And what kind of damage is all this doing?

Vlasov: Moonshine is extremely harmful and dangerous to health because, in addition to alcohol toxins, it contains a heavy concentration of highly poisonous fuel oils and spirits, metal oxides from the still, and all kinds of "special" additives—from tobacco to hydrochloric acid. In the last 18 months the militia has recorded 90 cases of group poisoning from alcohol substitutes. 200 people have died.

What other damage is caused by this problem? People become chronic alcoholics far more rapidly from moonshine, particularly teenagers . . . considerable economic damage is done, because valuable products—thousands of metric tons of sugar, beets, potatoes, and grain—are destroyed by being turned into toxic substances. The sharp increase in sugar sales in a number of regions of the country over the past year—a 14–16 per cent increase in Latvia and Moldavia, for example, and a 20 per cent increase in Kirghizia—require serious analysis, in particular.

Moonshiners often manufacture their "product" from stolen raw materials. The theft of sugar, grain, and beets for the purpose of unrefined vodka production has increased. A criminal group, led by the director of the Merkensky sugar refinery, which had embezzled sugar to the value of 140,000 rubles, has been broken up in Dzhambul, for example.

Moonshining has become a source of unearned income

and illegal gain. In Kursk oblast citizen Korolkova systematically manufactured and sold hooch at the Kastornaya-Novaya station. She was found to be in possession of 1.5 metric tons of home-brewed beer. The court confiscated a Zhiguli car bought with dishonest "earnings" and also a large amount of money. . . . Tens of litres of unrefined vodka, 0.5 metric ton of sugar, and approximately 20,000 rubles were confiscated from the inveterate moonshiner Arzamasova. . . . The unrefined vodka profiteers are being identified and face inevitable punishment.

The Result of Social Ills

Correspondent: Why are people now joining the "clan" of moonshiners when they formerly had no such intention?

Vlasov: There can be no serious talk of combating drunkenness and moonshining until the matters of improving the organization of people's work and leisure time and satisfying popular demand for services and consumer goods are resolved alongside or, to be more precise, in close conjunction with this problem.

It is a well-known fact that in rural areas a bottle of moonshine is often the main form of payment for all manner of services rendered on the side. Have a bottle ready if you need firewood transported, your garden dug, or your house repaired. In Tula oblast, for example, more than half of all those sentenced for selling moonshine had manufactured it to pay for consumer services.

Correspondent: Would you please tell us about the role of the militia in the fight against moonshining?

Vlasov: It must be admitted that the militia has proved ill-prepared for the outbreak of moonshining, particularly in the cities. We are now making up for lost time. But we have not been sitting idle, of course. A number of measures have been implemented. In the last 18 months approximately 900,000 illicit stills have been either voluntarily handed in or confiscated and 2–6 million litres of home-brewed beer and moonshine have been destroyed. Since the change in legislative norms, the number of charges brought across the country as a whole has increased 2–6 times. Over the past year more than 130,000 people have been found guilty by civil courts and 70,000 have been punished.

These are strong measures. They are evidence of a more active fight against bootlegging and moonshine. This evil is not becoming less prevalent, however—on the contrary, in many regions of the country it is growing. This shows up the inadequacy of the preventive measures taken with the participation of the public, and reveals one-sidedness and formality in applying the punishments laid down by the law. The greater number of penalties cannot be automatically identified with the effectiveness of anti-alcohol measures. In some areas MVD [Ministry of Internal Affairs] organs are dazzled by figures showing a rise in punishments and have clearly slackened their preventive efforts.

I must say that the malicious moonshiner has rapidly reorganized his activity, has gone deep underground, so to speak, and is mastering new techniques. In the village of Grishentsy in Vinnitsa oblast the militia caught a certain V. Postupaylo, who had set up a distillery in a forest thicket with a watchtower so that he could keep a look out with a pair of binoculars. . . . In Khoyniksky rayon, Gomel oblast, they discovered a centre for the collective production of unrefined vodka; several families took it in turns to tend it.

Religion Goes Underground

Dmitry S. Likhachev

Historically, the Russian people have been devout followers of the Russian Orthodox Church, a branch of Christianity similar to Greek Orthodoxy. The leaders of the Church, who are called metropolitans and who perform the same role as archbishops, were all appointed by the tsars. In turn, the metropolitans gave legitimacy to the tsar's rule. When the Communists came to power in 1917, it quickly became clear that, in order to destroy the power of the tsar, it was also necessary to destroy the power of the metropolitans. The persecution of the Russian Orthodox Church began shortly thereafter, and it intensified after Josef Stalin came to power in 1924. By 1930, most church congregations had either disbanded or gone underground.

After many years as a Soviet political prisoner, Dmitry S. Likhachev became a noted Russian literary and cultural historian. He was a student at the University of Leningrad in the late 1920s. In this selection from his memoirs, he recounts how a small intellectual circle to which he belonged reacted to the religious persecutions. He also describes how the state went about suppressing religion.

Right up to the end of 1927 [Leningrad] seethed with various philosophical circles, student societies and 'at homes' held by well-known people. People came together in the University, the Geographical Society and in their own

Dmitry S. Likhachev, *Reflections on the Russian Soul: A Memoir*, edited by A.R. Tulloch, translated by Bernard Adams. New York: Central European University Press, 2000.

homes. A range of problems—philosophical, historical and literary—were discussed. Students of literature split into *formalists*, representatives of the formal school, and those who maintained traditional methods of literary study. Disputes took place both in private circles and on official territory—in Leningrad University, in the Institute of the History of the Arts (the *Zubovski*) on St. Isaac's Square, but mostly in the hall of the Tenishevski college. We had our circles in the Lentovskaya school as well and one of them met in the flat of our teacher I.M. Andreyevski from the very beginning of the 20s. . . .

At meetings a huge book was passed around for people to sign, and at the top of the page the subject of the paper, the date and the speaker's name were written in Andreyevski's distinctive Gothic hand. . . .

The papers were on the most varied topics—literary, philosophical and theological. Discussions were lively and Andreyevski's little rooms were never empty.

Andreyevski had a huge and carefully selected library (at that time books were very cheap, and could be bartered for bread, salt, flour or even for things sold by weight!) We were all allowed to help ourselves from his library, even in his absence, so long as we stuck a note acknowledging the loan on a special spike, and didn't keep the book longer than the allotted time. Thanks to this library I managed to become acquainted with the most varied philosophical literature while still at school: and even if I couldn't read a certain book, it was important to just hold it in my hands, to memorise the list of contents and its external appearance and simply to discover its existence. . . .

Libraries and cultural circles were the basis of my education.

A Cultural Circle Becomes a Religious "Brotherhood"

In the second half of the 20s Andreyevski's circle . . . began to assume a more and more religious character. This change was no doubt explained by the persecutions to which the

Church was subject at the time. Discussion of Church affairs took up most of the circle's time. Andreyevski began to consider the change in the circle's fundamental leanings and tried to find it a new name. All were agreed that the circle, which several members of an atheistic tendency had by now left, should be called a 'brotherhood'. But named after whom? Andreyevski wanted to call it 'The Brotherhood of Metropolitan Filipp', having in mind Metropolitan Filipp Kolichëv, who told Ivan the Terrible the truth to his face and was strangled. . . . Then, however, under the influence of [S.A.] Alekseyev-Askoldov [one of the circle's members] we called it 'The Brotherhood of St Serafim of Sarov'.[1]

In the quarrel that broke out in 1927 between the supporters of Sergey and the intransigent Josefans, we, the young intelligentsia, were to a man on the side of Metropolitan Iosif, who had refused to recognise the declaration of Metropolitan Sergey, in which he had stated that there was not and had not been any persecution of the Church.[2]

The actions of the government with regard to the Church were plain for all to see: churches were being closed and desecrated, services were interrupted by the arrival of lorries with bands playing or spontaneous *Komsomol* [Young Communist League] choirs singing to a bold Gipsy tune a song composed by Demyan Bedny or someone of the sort, with the refrain:

Hunt them, hunt them down, the monks,
Hunt them, hunt them down, the priests,
Make those speculators run,
Crush the *kulaks* . . .

Komsomol members would pour into churches wearing their hats, talking in loud voices and laughing. I don't mean to list everything that was done at that time in the spiritual

1. St. Serafim of Sarov (1759–1833) was one of the best-known and best-loved spiritual teachers in the Russian Orthodox tradition. 2. Sergey, metropolitan of Nizhni-Novgorod, was made Patriarch, or leader, of the Russian Orthodox Church in return for his support of Soviet authority over the faithful. Iosif, metropolitan of Leningrad, refused to recognize Sergey's supremacy and rejected Soviet authority.

life of the nation but even the young Jewish intelligentsia were deeply embarrassed by events. My friend Misha Shapiro, who was of a Jewish family of the patriarchal faith, was upset and occasionally went to the chapel in one old people's home where there was a surprisingly good choir.

The Brotherhood Gets Infiltrated

We had the idea of going to church as a group. One day in 1927 five or six of us went together to one of the churches (later destroyed) in the Petrograd District. We were joined by Ionkin, who was an *agent provocateur* although we did not realise it at the time. He pretended to be religious but didn't know how to behave in church; he was nervous, hung back and stood behind us. At that point I began to have my doubts about him. But then it turned out that the appearance in church of a group of adults unknown to the parishioners caused alarm to the clergy, all the more so as Ionkin was carrying a briefcase. With that our 'group visits' ceased.

When I look back over those years I'm certain that we couldn't have had any other approach to the schism in the church than the emotional one. We were on the side of the persecuted Church and simply couldn't have brought ourselves to make the rational compromises to which part of the Orthodox episcopate was inclined. Had we been politicians, then we might have decided either way. But we weren't politicians fighting for the survival of the Church, merely believers who wanted to be honest in all things and were revolted by the political manoeuvrings, the programmes and the calculating, two-faced formulae that enabled people to avoid giving a straight answer.

I remember one day meeting the senior priest of the Preobrazhenski Cathedral, Father Sergi Tikhomirov . . . at my teacher's flat. He was extremely thin, with a sparse white beard. He was neither voluble nor loud of voice, and probably did his work quietly and humbly. When he was 'taken away' and asked about his views on Soviet power, he replied succinctly: "It's from the Antichrist". Obviously, he was arrested and very quickly shot. . . .

There were only three or four meetings of the Brotherhood before it was 'officially' closed. At one of the last of these Andreyevski introduced to us a young man who stood in front of us in the pose of the Apostle Bartholomew in Nesterov's well-known painting, clasping his hands together in an attitude of prayer and murmuring something unintelligible but 'inspired' and not addressing anyone in particular. Andreyevski went into raptures over him: "What a religious man, what a religious man!" Meanwhile the piggish eyes of the said 'religious man' were very watchful. As he greeted us he whispered "Serezha" and made an effort to learn the names and surnames of those present. A few days later I met him in the famous University corridor, where the long benches on which the students usually sat to argue over questions of politics and general philosophy had not yet been removed. One could meet a few students there at any time, such as, for example, the handsome Borya Ivanov, a convinced Kantian who later became an outstanding religious thinker.

I went up to 'Serezha' and engaged him in a conversation. As this conversation was drawing to a close he began trying to persuade me to help produce some kind of leaflets. "We'll leave them here in the corridor, and they'll be little fires, little fires, and a blaze will flare up. . ." I remember his using the words 'little fires' and 'blaze'. One of the students saw me talking to 'Serezha Ionkin' and warned me that he was an *agent provocateur.* In questioning me, Ionkin learned that my father had at one time taught chemistry in the no. 1 Nikolayevski cadet school. "I was a student of his . . . May I call on you?" I told my father. He replied "Ionkin? I remember all my students' surnames, but I never had one called Ionkin. . . ."

Then I went to see Andreyevski and warned him that our group had been infiltrated by an *agent provocateur.* It was decided that the Brotherhood should dissolve itself. The next Wednesday Ionkin was almost the first to arrive. Andreyevski met us with a frown, sat in a deep armchair upholstered in blue velvet which one of his pupils had given him, and began to speak of the futility of our meetings and his decision to meet no more. He called upon us all to go to whichever church our faith required as often as possible and to read religious literature, then he stood up and shook us all by the hand to say goodbye. Andreyevski's speech had been so convincing and, I might say, wise, that "Serezha Ionkin" believed it and left him in peace, but when he tried nevertheless to accost me in the University (he was at the time very drunk) I snubbed him with a decisiveness that was uncharacteristic of me at that age.

On looking over my dossier in 1992 I caught sight of the statements of one 'Ivanovski', and had no difficulty in identifying him as our Ionkin. 'Ivanovski' was a vile secret agent of the GPU [the Soviet secret police]. There is no evidence of his official position in my dossier, but his job of showing us all to be monarchists and raving counterrevolutionaries is clearly revealed. . . .

We didn't in fact meet at Andreyevski's for some time after the incident with the *agent provocateur.* It seems to me that [Andreyevski] was inclined to go over entirely to church affairs, and the diversity that was shown at the meetings . . . was becoming just a little inappropriate in the light of the events that the Russian Church was experiencing.

We couldn't, however, do without [Andreyevski] entirely. The need to exchange views on what was happening around us was too great. We would call uninvited at his flat, borrow his books as before, placing receipts on the big spike which was stuck into one of the shelves, and when we found him in we'd try to get his opinion on some affair or other, or listen to him talking about Church affairs. The circle shrank, naturally, but it did still exist, and [Andreyevski] obviously felt that he had no right to send us away. The meetings began again spontaneously.

The Brotherhood of Serafim Sarovski continued to exist until the day of our arrest, 8 February 1928.

Eliminating the Influence of the Church

William O. Douglas

Karl Marx once wrote that "religion is the opium of the people." Vladimir Lenin took this idea a step further by declaring that all good communists must also be atheists. Lenin hated the Russian Orthodox Church, the religious mainstay of Russians for centuries, because it had served as a prop to the Romanov dynasty. He also distrusted organized religion in general because it served as an alternative source of authority to the state. Under Lenin and later Josef Stalin, the Soviet government vigorously subverted religion.

In 1955, two years after Stalin's death, William O. Douglas, a U.S. Supreme Court justice, was allowed to tour the Soviet Union. Among other things, he discovered that the vast majority of people had abandoned the open practice of religion. He also found, however, that religious sentiment among Soviets was still surprisingly strong.

"We do not believe in religion. Religion is for backward people only." The speaker was Kaspov, the young Russian professor of the university in Frunze. . . . He faced me across the table in the office of the Rector, Dr. Unusaliev. Russian and Kirgiz faculty members filled the room where we sat. When Kaspov announced that religion is for " backward people only," I raised my right hand and said,

William O. Douglas, *Russian Journey*. New York: Doubleday, 1956.

"Then I'm a backward person." Kaspov instantly replied, "No insult was intended. I merely state our socialist point of view." . . .

When I pressed for a definition of "backward people," I was told that they are "the old people"—those too old to throw off their "bourgeois" or "capitalistic" philosophy. . . .

Separation of Church and State

Only in a limited sense are church and state separate in Russia. The state does not interfere with baptisms, burial services, prayers, singing, or any of the other rituals of the church. One may go to church without being fined or imprisoned; and the police do not break up church services. But in other respects the state applies powerful sanctions against the church.

—The Soviets confiscated all church property, taking title to all land and buildings. The churches occupy the property merely at the sufferance of the government.

—The church is not a juridical person in Soviet law. That is to say, the church cannot defend its property rights in the courts nor receive bequests under wills. (Soviet courts have winked at that prohibition by recognizing bequests made to ministers or priests.)

—The church is subject to the income tax, paying 13 per cent of all its revenues to the state.

—The youth of Russia are taught that religion is evil, that atheism is the true faith. These teachings are dinned into their ears, beginning with the nursery.

—The state has destroyed the pulpit, as we of the West know it. Today no priest, no minister would dare preach social justice from his pulpit, except and unless the social justice he championed fit precisely the Communist pattern.

—No person who belongs to a church can qualify for membership in the Communist party. No candidate for office, whether or not a party member, will be endorsed by the party, if he belongs to a church or is active in religious affairs. And a candidate without party backing has no chance of being elected. The churchman or churchgoer is, in other words, disqualified from every public post, whether it be alderman, mayor, or governor. (This is the rule and the general practice, though there are, I learned, some Communist members who are believers.)

These restraints are placed on all churches, whatever their creed.

Jews and Moslems

There is another which hits the Jews harshly. There is no possibility of staying away from work on the Jewish Sabbath, unless by chance the work week makes the holiday fall at that time. And there are two restraints of which the Moslems alone are victims. First, there is Ramadan, the month of fasting, when from sunrise to sunset the Moslems neither eat, drink, nor smoke. Ramadan is an exacting fast, one that can be successfully completed only if one slows down and receives some accommodation from his employer. There is no employer in Central Asia who will relax the party's strict demands. And so Ramadan as an institution has withered away.

Second, every Moslem desires to make at least one journey to Mecca during his lifetime. Once he makes the trip he is worthy to be called a *hajji*. The trip from Central Asia to Saudi Arabia is a long and arduous one for the average man. There are mountains to traverse and deserts to cross; and the trails are bitter cold in winter and blistering hot in summer. Nevertheless the faithful all through the centuries made their long treks to Mecca from the heart of Central Asia, hundreds of them going each year. When the Communists came to power and seized Central Asia as part of the Russian empire, they sealed the southern border. It is sealed to this day. No Moslem headed for Mecca can cross the border without a permit. Over the years the Soviets have granted very few.

During my visit to Soviet Central Asia, I talked with many of the Moslem clergy about these pilgrimages. The Soviet travel restrictions have, indeed, hit hard at them. There is no layman who has made the trip to Mecca since 1917. Only a few of the clergy have been granted the dispensation by the

Soviets. Many of the mullahs have never seen Mecca.

One day in Alma Ata, I talked with a group of mullahs about this problem. I had visited a mosque without an appointment. It was Friday, the Moslem Sunday; so the bulk of the congregation was present—perhaps a hundred people, all of whom were fifty years old or more and a third of whom were women. This mosque is not ornate like those one sees in Iran. It's an ordinary wooden building painted blue. Its distinctive feature is a graceful crescent high on the steeple. The churchyard is enclosed by a drab mud wall. The grounds were untidy, without grass, flowers, or shrubs. The interior of the church was as dreary as the yard. No artist had enlivened it. The walls and ceiling were as monotonous as the worn-out rugs where the faithful prayed.

I introduced myself to the head mullah. His brown eyes sparkled and his whole face lightened as I mentioned Mecca. This man of fifty-five years has been to Mecca once and that was in 1953. He told me how the Soviet Government in recent years has relaxed its restrictions—and worked out a quota system for pilgrims. The republic of Kazakhstan sends its quota every fourth year. During the intervening two years, the other four Central Asian republics send their quotas. I inquired how the quotas were determined. It appears that one pilgrimage plane a year is allowed to go from Baku to Teheran. The mullahs must, of course, pay for the plane. The length of their purses and the seating capacity of the plane determine the size of the quota. There were eighteen who went from Kazakhstan in 1953. It would be Kazakhstan's turn again in 1956.

The mullah, who related these facts to me, expressed gratitude to the Soviet Government for making the pilgrimages possible. This priest, like every clergyman I met in Russia, was docile in his attitude toward the state. Among the clergy I met, none ever gave any telltale evidence of dissatisfaction with the Soviet Government. Forty years under a Communist regime have taught them that the way to survive is to remain silent on controversial issues and never to speak in disparaging terms about the government.

Church Attendance

Churches built for large congregations often have meager attendance. I attended mass in an Armenian church in Baku where there were seven priests conducting the service and only four old women and one old man in the audience. In Bukhara, once a great center of Islamic learning, there is only one active mosque and it is in a state of disrepair. At one important service I saw less than twenty worshipers—and they were all old men. Bukhara once had many religious schools serving all of Central Asia. Today, as I said earlier, it has but one seminary with only 100 students in attendance. That is, indeed, the one and only Moslem training school in all of Central Asia.

There are over three million Jews in Russia and about two-hundred congregations. There are synagogues in most of the cities I visited. These congregations are active. But not many of the younger generation are being taught the precepts of Judaism. And the rabbis complain of the difficulty in getting cantors.

From Church to Museum

Everywhere in Russia one finds some old churches in ruins and others that have been turned into cinemas, warehouses, and museums. A magnificent mosque in Ashkhabad, capital of Turkmenistan, was partly demolished on October 6, 1948 by an earthquake that nearly destroyed the town. That mosque today stands in ruins, unrestored. Most of the mosques in Central Asia are in disrepair. Leningrad, which suffered heavily under German artillery, has rebuilt all her magnificent buildings—all except some of the churches that still carry the wounds of war.

All over Russia more and more churches are being turned into museums. The old churches of the czars within the walls of the Kremlin are now only famous show places. Like the throne of Ivan the Terrible, they are merely symbols of royalist days.

The famous Cathedral of the Virgin of Kazan in Leningrad has been converted into a museum dedicated to "The Evolution of Religion and Atheism." As one walks in he sees a picture of peasants carrying a golden cross, on top of which is a fat man with a cigar in his mouth and a whip in his hand. Christ is walking ahead in a golden robe. . . .

The Anti-Religion Campaign

In all of Russia the campaign against religion is incessant. It starts in the nursery and kindergarten that are found in every town and factory and on every farm.

They open at 7 A.M. and close either at 7 P.M. or 8 P.M. They are dependable, efficient, and free. They not only make it possible for mother to work; they also put the child in the hands of the state during his early years. He stays in a kindergarten until he enters public school at the age of seven. During these first seven years the nurses tune the ear of the child to atheism, not to God.

A Jesuit maxim says, "Give me a child for the first seven years, and you may do what you like with him afterwards." Lenin in 1923 rephrased that maxim to read: "Give us a child for eight years and it will be a Bolshevist forever." The nurseries and kindergartens of Soviet Russia are dedicated to Lenin's creed.

The atheistic influence does not end there. A child from the time he is seven until he reaches fourteen usually has a chance to go to a Pioneer camp during the summer months. That again is free to the children. The ones I saw are healthful places in the physical sense, being located in the mountains, on lakes or rivers, or in the country. At these camps there are games and sports, music and dancing, and other group activities. But there are also classes in reading and storytelling. The library is filled only with Communist literature. I saw and heard enough to know that all libraries and discussion groups open to children are barren of any religious influence and interest the mind only in material things.

The anti-religious campaign extends to the adults as well as to the children. That campaign is no longer a police action. As Khrushchev said in the fall of 1955, "Our anti-religious campaigns are done by the written word or through discussion and argument." The campaign goes on even though the severest critics of the church concede that today there is no "class basis" of religion in Russia.

Literature available either at sidewalk bookstalls or at libraries is non-religious and often outright anti-religious. If there are great religious classics in Russia, they are buried deep in rare-book collections of the libraries. The slant of the Soviet press is anti-religious. And if the press is lax, some party member speaks up to remind the government to liquidate all "religious survivals." In a myriad of ways the state has done its best to liquidate them. When witnesses are sworn in court, "So help me God" is not included in the oath.

The Persistence of Faith

Though the churches have suffered a great setback under the Communists, they are still strong. In the larger cities such as Moscow and Leningrad, the people turn out by the hundreds for services. On holy days, such as Easter, the crowds that pack the cathedrals run into the thousands. At Alma Ata, 3000 people attended the various masses at the Russian Orthodox church on the Sunday in August 1955 when I visited there.

The Catholic service is the same in Moscow as in America. The Russian Orthodox church too has a rich ritual; and it puts great stress on miracles and the life hereafter. The Protestant pulpit, though not designed for Henry Ward Beecher, is still active. The sermons are partly theological essays (usually of the fundamentalist type) and partly dissertations on the life of Christ, His teachings, and the inspiration of His example.

Though the church does not have the hold on people that it once had, the nexus is not broken. I saw young people bringing their babies to church for baptism in the Catholic church of St. Louis in Moscow and in the Russian Orthodox churches all the way across Russia. I mentioned earlier that the synagogues were not indoctrinating the youth in the principles of Judaism as they did before. But the old rituals continue; and the ceremony of the confirmation (bar mitzvah) is still a vital one. For example, at the Choral Synagogue in Moscow, which has a congregation of perhaps ten thousand Jews, about twenty boys receive their confirmation every month.

Every church is still popular for marriages.

The church also remains a favorite place for burial services. The state does not provide many undertakers; and there are few funeral parlors. Private enterprise in that field is not allowed. And so one must provide his own hearse. The funeral service in Russia is, therefore, marked by the coffin carried on a pickup truck.

Birth, marriage, and death—these are the great milestones of life. They are events to commemorate with solemnity and dignity. No matter what the party may say, it cannot compete with the church on these occasions. The church has a ritual steeped in symbolism. No party can rob it of its charm. The church, as a mother institution, will be there long after the party has changed its spots.

Putting Work Before Marriage and Love

Alexandra Kollontai

Alexandra Kollontai was the world's first woman ambassador. She served as the Soviet Union's minister to Norway (1923–1925, 1927–1930), Mexico (1925–1927), and Sweden (1930–1945). She was also the Soviet Union's first People's Commissar of Social Welfare; her closest U.S. counterpart would be the Secretary of Health, Education, and Welfare. In this capacity she effected the passage of laws making it easier for women to obtain divorces, granting equal treatment to illegitimate children and their mothers, and involving women more completely in the arenas of society and government. As a result of her efforts and those of like-minded women, Soviet women were afforded opportunities to enter professions and to play active roles in government.

Kollontai outraged many Russians, including a number of her fellow communists, by advocating sexual relations between consenting adults outside of marriage, the raising of children by the state rather than the parents, and the total equality of women to men within marriage. In this selection from her 1926 autobiography, she outlines her involvement in the women's liberation movement during the formative years of Soviet communism.

I am still far from being the type of the positively new women who take their experience as females with a relative lightness and, one could say, with an enviable superfi-

Alexandra Kollontai, *The Autobiography of a Sexually Emancipated Communist Woman*, edited by Iring Fetscher, translated by Salvator Attanasio. New York: Herder and Herder, 1971.

ciality, whose feelings and mental energies are directed upon all other things in life but sentimental love feelings. After all I still belong to the generation of women who grew up at a turning point in history. Love with its many disappointments, with its tragedies and eternal demands for perfect happiness still played a very great role in my life. An all-too-great role! It was an expenditure of precious time and energy, fruitless and, in the final analysis, utterly worthless. We, the women of the past generation, did not yet understand how to be free. The whole thing was an absolutely incredible squandering of our mental energy, a diminution of our labor power which was dissipated in barren emotional experiences. It is certainly true that we, myself as well as many other activists, militants and working women contemporaries, were able to understand that love was not the main goal of our life and that we knew how to place work at its center. Nevertheless we would have been able to create and achieve much more had our energies not been fragmentized in the eternal struggle with our egos and with our feelings for another. It was, in fact, an eternal defensive war against the intervention of the male into our ego, a struggle revolving around the problem-complex: work or marriage and love? We, the older generation, did not yet understand, as most men do and as young women are learning today, that work and the longing for love can be harmoniously combined so that work remains as the main goal of existence. Our mistake was that each time we succumbed to the belief that we had finally found the one and only in the man we loved, the person with whom we believed we could blend our soul, one who was ready fully to recognize us as a spiritual-physical force.

But over and over again things turned out differently, since the man always tried to impose his ego upon us and adapt us fully to his purposes. Thus despite everything the inevitable inner rebellion ensued, over and over again since love became a fetter. We felt enslaved and tried to loosen the love-bond. And after the eternally recurring struggle with the beloved man, we finally tore ourselves away and rushed toward freedom. Thereupon we were again alone, unhappy, lonesome, but free—free to pursue our beloved, chosen ideal . . . work.

Fortunately young people, the present generation, no longer have to go through this kind of struggle which is absolutely unnecessary to human society. Their abilities, their work-energy will be reserved for their creative activity. Thus the existence of barriers will become a spur. . . .

Receiving Her Post

[In 1917] the Soviet Government was formed. I was appointed People's Commissar (Minister) of Social Welfare. I was the only woman in the cabinet and the first woman in history who had ever been recognized as a member of a government. When one recalls the first months of the Workers' Government, months which were so rich in magnificent illusions, plans, ardent initiatives to improve life, to organize the world anew, months of the real romanticism of the Revolution, one would in fact like to write about all else save about one's self. I occupied the post of Minister of Social Welfare from October of 1917 to March of 1918. It was not without opposition that I was received by the former officials of the Ministry. Most of them sabotaged us openly and simply did not show up for work. But precisely this office could not interrupt its work, come what may, since in itself it was an extraordinarily complicated operation. It included the whole welfare program for the war-disabled, hence for hundreds of thousands of crippled soldiers and officers, the pension system in general, foundling homes, homes for the aged, orphanages, hospitals for the needy, the work-shops making artificial limbs, the administration of playing-card factories (the manufacture of playing cards was a State monopoly), the educational system, clinical hospitals for women. In addition a whole series of educational institutes for young girls were also under the direction of this Ministry. One can easily imagine the enormous demands these tasks made upon a small group of people who, at the same time, were novices in State administration. In a clear awareness of these difficulties I formed, immediately, an auxiliary council in which experts such as physicians, jurists, pedagogues were represented alongside the workers and the minor officials of the Ministry. The sacrifice, the energy with which the minor employees bore the burden of this difficult task was truly exemplary. It was not only a matter of keeping the work of the Ministry going, but also of initiating reforms and improvements. New, fresh forces replaced the sabotaging officers of the old regime. A new life stirred in the offices of the formerly highly conservative Ministry. Days of grueling work! And at night the sessions of the councils of the People's Commissar (of the cabinet) under Lenin's chairmanship. A small, modest room and only one secretary who recorded the resolutions which changed Russia's life to its bottommost foundations. . . .

The Work

My main work as People's Commissar consisted in the following: by decree to improve the situation of the war-disabled, to abolish religious instruction in the schools for young girls which were under the Ministry (this was still before the general separation of Church and State), and to transfer priests to the civil service, to introduce the right of self-administration for pupils in the schools for girls, to reorganize the former orphanages into government Children's Homes (no distinction was to be made between orphaned children and those who still had fathers and mothers), to set up the first hostels for the needy and street-urchins, to convene a committee, composed only of doctors, which was to be commissioned to elaborate the free public health system for the whole country. In my opinion the most important accomplishment of the People's Commissariat, however, was the legal foundation of a Central Office for Maternity and Infant Welfare. The draft of the bill relating to this Central Office was signed by me in January of 1918. A second decree followed in which I changed all maternity hospitals into free Homes for Maternity and Infant Care, in order thereby to set the groundwork for a comprehensive government system of pre-natal care. I was greatly assisted in coping with these tasks by Dr. Korolef. We also planned a "Pre-Natal Care Palace," a model home with an exhibition room in which

Sexual Restraint: Good for Capitalists, Bad for Communists

One of Alexandra Kollontai's most controversial essays was "Theses on Communist Morality in the Sphere of Marital Relations." Among other things, it argued that communism made the family obsolete, that a Communist woman must do more than fall in love and devote herself to her husband and children, and that men and women should be free to engage in sexual relations without regard for bourgeois morality. In this excerpt, she asserts that sexual relations are essential to the well-being of healthy and productive workers.

In the period of the dictatorship of the proletariat relations between the sexes should be evaluated only according to the following criteria—the health of the working population and the development of inner bonds of solidarity within the collective. The sexual act must not be seen as something shameful and sinful but as something which is as natural as the other needs of [a] healthy organism, such as hunger and thirst. Such phenomena cannot be judged as moral or immoral. The satisfaction of healthy and natural instincts only ceases to be normal when the boundaries of hygiene are overstepped. . . . As communist morality is concerned for the health of the population, it also criticises sexual restraint. The preservation of health includes the full and correct satisfaction of all man's needs; norms of hygiene should work to this end, and not artificially suppress such an important function of the organism as the sex drive. Thus both early sexual experience (before the body has developed and grown strong) and sexual restraint must be seen as equally harmful.

Alexandra Kollontai, *Selected Writings of Alexandra Kollontai.* Translated with an introduction and commentaries by Alix Holt. New York: Lawrence Hill Books, 1977.

courses for mothers would be held and, among many other things, model day nurseries were also to be established. . . .

My efforts to nationalize maternity and infant care set off a new wave of insane attacks against me. All kinds of lies were related about the "nationalization of women," about my legislative proposals which assertedly ordained that little girls of 12 were to become mothers. A special fury gripped the religious followers of the old regime when, on my own authority (the cabinet later criticized me for this action), I transformed the famous Alexander Nevsky monastery into a home for war-invalids. The monks resisted and a shooting fray ensued. The press again raised a loud hue and cry against me. The Church organized street demonstrations against my action and also pronounced "anathema" against me. . . .

I received countless threatening letters, but I never requested military protection. I always went out alone, unarmed and without any kind of a bodyguard. In fact I never gave a thought to any kind of danger, being all too engrossed in matters of an utterly different character. In February of 1918 a first State delegation of the Soviets was sent to Sweden in order to clarify different economic and political questions. As People's Commissar I headed this delegation. . . .

Women's Liberation

The first Congress of Women Workers and Women Peasants [was] called [in] November of 1918; some 1147 delegates were present. Thus the foundation was laid for methodical work in the whole country for the liberation of the women of the working and the peasant classes. A flood of new work was waiting for me. The question now was one of drawing women into the people's kitchens and of educating them to devote their energies to children's homes and day-care centers, the school system, household reforms, and still many other pressing matters. The main thrust of all this activity was to implement, in fact, equal rights for women as a labor unit in the national economy and as a citizen in the political sphere and, of course, with the special proviso: maternity was to be appraised as a social function and therefore protected and provided for by the State. . . . At same time, central officers were established in the whole country to deal with issues and tasks connected with women's liberation and to draw women into Soviet work.

The Civil War in 1919 saddled me with new tasks. When the White troops [Russians who fought against the Bolshevik revolution] tried to march north from south Russia, I was again sent to the Ukraine and to the Crimea where at first I served as chairwoman of the enlightenment department in the Army. Later, up to the evacuation of the Soviet government, I was appointed People's Commissar of Enlightenment and Propaganda in the Ukrainian government. I managed to send 400 women communists out of the threatened zone near Kiev with a special train. I did my most possible best for the communist women-workers movement also in the Ukraine.

A serious illness tore me away from the exciting work for months. Hardly having recovered—at that time I was in Moscow—I took over the direction of the Coordinating Office for Work among Women and again a new period of intensive, grueling work began. A communist women's newspaper was founded, conferences and congresses of women workers were convoked. The foundation was laid for work with the women of the East [Muslims]. Two world conferences of communist women took place in Moscow. The law liberalizing abortion was put through and a number of regulations of benefit to women were introduced by our Coordinating Office and legally confirmed. At this time I had to do more writing and speaking than ever before. . . . Our work received wholehearted support from Lenin. And Trotsky, although he was overburdened with military tasks, unfailingly and gladly appeared at our conferences. Energetic, gifted women . . . sacrificially devoted all their energies to the work of the Coordinating Office.

At the eighth Soviet Congress, as a member of the Soviet executive (now there were already several women on this body), I proposed a motion that the Soviets in all areas contribute to the creation of a consciousness of the struggle for equal rights for women and, accordingly, to involve them in

State and communal work. I managed to push the motion through and to get it accepted but not without resistance. It was a great, an enduring victory.

A heated debate flared up when I published my thesis on the new morality. For our Soviet marriage law, separated from the Church to be sure, is not essentially more progressive than the same laws that after all exist in other progressive democratic countries. Although the illegitimate child was placed on a legal par with the legitimate child, in practice a great deal of hypocrisy and injustice still exists in this area. When one speaks of the "immorality" which the Bolsheviks purportedly propagated, it suffices to submit our marriage laws to a close scrutiny to note that in the divorce question we are on a par with North America whereas in the question of the illegitimate child we have not yet even progressed as far as the Norwegians.

The most radical wing of the Party was formed around this question. My theses, my sexual and moral views, were bitterly fought by many Party comrades of both sexes: as were still other differences of opinion in the Party regarding political guiding principles. Personal and family cares were added thereto and thus months in 1922 went by without fruitful work. Then in the autumn of 1922 came my official appointment to the legation of the Russian Soviet representation in Norway. I really believed that this appointment would be purely formal and that therefore in Norway I would find time to devote to myself, to my literary activity. Things turned out quite differently. With the day of my entry into office in Norway I also entered upon a wholly new course of work in my life which drew upon all my energies to the highest degree. . . .

I took up my duties in Norway in October of 1922 and as early as 1923 the head of the legation went on holiday so that I had officially to conduct the affairs of the Soviet Republic for him. Soon thereafter, however, I was appointed as the representative of my country in his stead. Naturally this appointment created a great sensation since, after all, it was the first time in history that a woman was officially active as an "ambassador." The conservative press and especially the Russian "White" press were outraged and tried to make a real monster of immorality and a bloody bogy out of me. Now especially a profusion of articles were written about my "horrid views" in relation to marriage and love. Nevertheless I must stress here that it was only the conservative press that gave me such an unfriendly reception in my new position. In all the social relations which I had during the three years of my work in Norway, I never once experienced the least trace of aversion or mistrust against woman's capabilities. To be sure, the healthy, democratic spirit of the Norwegian people greatly contributed to this. Thus the fact is to be confirmed that my work as official Russian representative in Norway was never, and in no wise, made difficult for the reason that I belonged "to the weaker sex." In connection with my position as ambassadress I also had to assume the duties of a Trade Plenipotentiary of the Russian governmental trade representation in Norway. Naturally both tasks in their special way were new to me. Nevertheless I set myself the task of effecting the de jure [legal] recognition of Soviet Russia and of re-establishing normal trade relations between the two countries which had been broken by the war and the revolution. The work began with great zeal and the most roseate hopes. A splendid summer and an eventful winter marked the year of 1923! The newly resumed trade relations were in full swing: Russian corn and Norwegian herring and fish, Russian wood products and Norwegian paper and cellulose. On February 15, 1924, Norway in fact recognized the U.S.S.R. de jure. I was appointed "chargé d'affaires" and officially introduced into the diplomatic corps. Now negotiations for a trade treaty between the two countries began. My life was crammed with strenuous work and highly interesting experiences alike. I had also to settle grave questions connected with the further development of trade and of shipping. After several months, in August of 1924, I was appointed "Ministre Plenipotentiere" and handed over my warrant to the king of Norway with the usual ceremonial. This, of course, gave the conservative press of all countries another occasion to spew their invectives upon me. After all, never before in all history had a woman been accepted as ambassador with the customary pomp and ceremony.

The trade agreement was concluded in Moscow at the end of 1925 and in February I countersigned the ratified treaty in Oslo with the president of the Norwegian cabinet, I.L. Mowickl.

The signing marked the successful accomplishment of my whole mission in Norway. I could hasten towards new goals and for this reason I left my post in Norway.

If I have attained something in this world, it was not my personal qualities that originally brought this about. Rather my achievements are only a symbol of the fact that woman, after all, is already on the march to general recognition. It is the drawing of millions of women into productive work, which was swiftly effected especially during the war and which thrust into the realm of possibility the fact that a woman could be advanced to the highest political and diplomatic positions. Nevertheless it is obvious that only a country of the future, such as the Soviet Union, can dare to confront woman without any prejudice, to appraise her only from the standpoint of her skills and talents, and, accordingly, to entrust her with responsible tasks. Only the fresh revolutionary storms were strong enough to sweep away hoary prejudices against woman and only the productive-working people is able to effect the complete equalization and liberation of woman by building a new society.

As I now end this autobiography, I stand on the threshold of new missions and life is making new demands upon me. . . .

No matter what further tasks I shall be carrying out, it is perfectly clear to me that the complete liberation of the working woman and the creation of the foundation of a new sexual morality will always remain the highest aim of my activity, and of my life.

Chapter 5

Making Communism Work

Chapter Preface

The biggest challenge faced by the Soviets was building a successful socialist economy. To this end, three major problems had to be overcome. Managers had to learn how to meet the demands of a planned economy. Workers had to be encouraged to increase productivity. Troublemakers and incompetents had to be rooted out before they could wreck the system.

In the Soviets' planned economy, the only "customer" was the government. In theory, trained economic planners determined how much of each commodity the various industries and factories would produce, and then allocated the resources required to meet the plan, thus assuring that all of the nation's needs were met. In reality, many planners were Communist Party bureaucrats who had no training in the industry for which they were responsible. Many plans called for unrealistically high production quotas, particularly in light of the fact that the demand for raw materials always exceeded the supply. As a result, managers often were forced to meet their quotas by producing as much as possible without any regard for the quality of the product, falsifying production records, and obtaining a sufficient supply of raw materials via bribery and black marketeering.

The more adept managers became at using bribery and record-falsification, the harder the government worked to expose such practices. As in the West, one of the leading institutions in the fight against corruption was the media. Incompetent and corrupt superiors were often reported to the nation's leading newspapers, which conducted investigations and reported the results. Surprisingly often, these reports spurred government officials to take action against such managers, even ones who were ranking members of the Communist Party.

In the early days of the Soviet Union, most workers were willing to make the necessary sacrifices to build the "workers' paradise." As time went on, however, and the workers' paradise failed to materialize, it became more difficult to get workers to toil long hours under stressful conditions without gaining significant material rewards. Resourceful managers resorted to ingenious solutions, such as building championship sports teams, to boost worker morale and productivity.

The great fear of Soviet officials was that many Soviet citizens had remained unreconstructed bourgeois capitalists who desired nothing better than to wreck the socialist system from within. In their zeal to root out and destroy such persons, the authorities imprisoned thousands of innocent people. Just as bad, the relatives of "wreckers," even those who were not accused of aiding and abetting them, were treated as if they, too, were wreckers. One of the saddest plights in Soviet history was the fate of "criminals without crimes," as the relatives of wreckers came to be known.

Criminals Without Crimes

Zinaida Cherkovskaya

One of the most unfortunate aspects of life under Soviet communism was the treatment of "criminals without crimes," the relatives of political outcasts. Although these people had done nothing wrong, they were tainted by their relationships with those who had been found guilty of trying to sabotage communism. Quite often, the relatives were treated as if they themselves had committed the crimes of which their loved ones had been convicted.

Zinaida Cherkovskaya was a young woman whose ex-husband was exiled after being found guilty of "wrecking," or sabotaging, the development of communism. Later, she fell in love with P.A. Melnikov, a rising star in the Smolensk branch of the Communist Party (CPSU). But because Cherkovskaya had once been married to a wrecker, even though she had left him before his conviction, Melnikov was ordered by the Party to have nothing more to do with her. This selection is a letter written in 1936 by her to Ivan P. Rumyantsev, one of Melnikov's superiors in the Party, begging Rumyantsev to allow the two lovers to renew their romance.

Ivan Petrovich:

The matter about which I have decided to write you concerns the CPSU(b) member Melnikov, who works with you in the Obkom [governing committee]. In the investigation of Party documents he received a reprimand because of

Merle Fainsod, *Smolensk Under Soviet Rule*. Cambridge, MA: Harvard University Press, 1958.

me, and because of this my life has been completely shattered, and therefore I cannot remain silent. I feel that I should write you everything frankly and honestly.

An Unhappy First Marriage

I am the daughter of a railroad employee. My father worked on the railroad for 35 years, 25 years at Pochinok Station, Western Oblast [a political division of a state]. A few years ago, at the age of 17, I married a veterinarian, who, upon finishing the institute, was assigned to Pochinok. It may have been because he was twice as old as I, or for another reason, but from the first days of our life together it became obvious that we had nothing in common, we were different types of people, strangers. At first I did not have enough resoluteness to speak of divorce, and then a baby came and I lived for the greater part of a year with my parents in Pochinok. When my husband was transferred to the Brasov stud farm, I started to study at the Brasov technical school, and he at the same time found himself a more suitable woman and began to live with her, although unofficially. I did not finish the technical school, because I did not want to live where he was, and I went to Moscow for a half-year course, leaving my daughter with my mother. After finishing the course, I returned to Pochinok and remained there to take care of my sick mother, who died within a year. From the moment I left Brasov I had no correspondence with my former husband. He lived openly with another woman, but no one in Pochinok, except my parents, knew that we had separated. I was ashamed to talk about it. In 1932 I learned that he had been arrested for participation in a wreckers' organization and was exiled for 3 years. When things went badly with him he remembered me and our daughter and began to write, to beg forgiveness, etc. I never loved him, and after all this he didn't mean anything to me at all, but for the sake of our daughter I agreed to write him once in a while about her. After the death of my mother I continued to live with my daughter and my father in Pochinok. I began to work as a proofreader in the editorial office of the *Pochinok*

Kolkhoznik. I worked enthusiastically, felt free, independent, wanted very much to live, wanted happiness, which I had never known. After a time Melnikov was appointed editor of the *P.K.* We became acquainted and liked each other. We began to see each other. On the first night I told him everything about myself, so that there would be no misunderstandings afterwards. I'm not going to begin to speak about him, but I fell head over heels in love with him. After some time, we became intimate.

Rejected by Her Lover

Soon he was appointed assistant secretary of the raikom [political division similar to a county] of the CPSU(b), and under the pretext that he had a great deal of work, we began to see each other less often, and after a time I was dismissed from work. It was Melnikov who did this, since there was not yet a new editor. It is impossible to express in words how I suffered. I had put my whole soul into my work, heard only approval from those around me, and the man who knew me best of all dismissed me from work. Often I was insistently pursued by the thought of suicide. This is cowardice, I know, but I felt that it was easier to die than to live without the man in whom I saw all happiness, all joy for myself. My little daughter forced me to dispel these thoughts.

I went to Smolensk and got a job as a proofreader in the House of the Press, and although I was the youngest proofreader, they soon appointed me copy editor on the kolkhoz [Soviet collective farm] newspaper. Soon Melnikov began to study in the Institute of Marxism-Leninism, and we met and spent our free time together, but he lived in the dormitory and I with my sister, since it was difficult to find a room in which to live together, and furthermore, it was easier and better for him to study while living with his fellow students. We lived in the hope that after he finished his studies we would finally settle things. But in the fall of 1935 I learned that they had created a whole case against Melnikov because he was seeing me. We began to see each other less frequently, and finally parted. Later I learned that they had reprimanded him because of me. I do not know to this day of what I was accused—nobody told me. But I was completely devoted to Melnikov, lived for his interests, and the fact that he had unpleasantness on account of me was painful and incomprehensible to me. My position was desperate.

After working a year in the House of the Press, I left work in August, as Melnikov had suggested. When I learned of his reprimand, I went to pieces. It seemed to me that not only had I no right to work, but that I could not live with people. I left my sister without telling her the reason, and I did not want to live with my father. I feared that there would be unpleasantness for him on account of me, although he was in the decline of life.

In January 1936 I received a letter from my former husband, in which he wrote that they had freed him before his term was up and that he had worked for a year in the system of the NKVD [The Soviet secret police] in Kazakhstan. At the end he wrote: if during these four years you did not get married, during your vacation come to visit me with your daughter, to see Kazakhstan. At that time I could not reason sensibly. I decided that my life was at an end anyway, and I went to him with my daughter, but I could not live with him for one day. I told him I had loved somebody else for three years now, and that only despair could have pushed me to this rash journey. He decided that I had sacrificed myself for the sake of my daughter. He really does not know the situation, and I did not want to tell him. He hopes that sometime I will "quiet down" and will be able to live with him. In April he went to a health resort and I went to my relatives in Smolensk. I am not deceived in regard to him. I am not a young girl. I am 24 years old and have lived through many adversities of life, and things were good with me only with Melnikov. I will not be able to fall out of love with him or forget him, and I never want to build my life without him. I met him accidentally in Smolensk, told him how much I had suffered without him, and he told me that I should live only in my work, but that we should not see each other.

"I Think I Shall Go Mad"

But I think I shall go mad. I don't want to be reconciled to it. I cannot get it through my head that in our free country, where the children of kulaks [peasants who possess above average wealth]* are not responsible for the crimes of their parents, I should be tortured my whole life because my former husband was once sentenced, and I do not have the right to be the wife of the man I love. Though he is a Party member, I am not an alien. I have concealed nothing, I have deceived no one, and I do not want to be a criminal without a crime.

I have recounted my whole life and all my "crimes" to you, Ivan Petrovich, more frankly than to my own father. At the cost of my life I would be happy to prove to you the truthfulness of my words.

I trust you implicitly, and whatever your opinion will be on this problem, it will be law for me.

ZINAIDA CHERKOVSKAYA

* During the 1920s, the kulaks were persecuted by Stalin, and their children were treated as "criminals without crimes."

A Whistleblower Gets Results

G. Zinkevich

The most difficult problem faced by the Soviet economy was production. One reason was that the production quotas set at the national level were often so unrealistically high that many upper-level managers were forced to manipulate the numbers in order to keep their jobs. In time, some managers resorted to this type of deceipt as a way to keep from doing their jobs. Although "fudging the numbers" became a generally accepted practice, many managers frowned upon the practice because it impeded the progress of socialism.

G. Zinkevich was the chief economist at a Soviet state farm near Kiev in the Ukraine. In 1981 she wrote to the editors of *Pravda*, a highly respected Soviet newspaper, to expose quota manipulation on the part of the farm's managers and their protection by the district executive committee of the Communist Party. The letter prompted an investigation by the newspaper, which led to an investigation by the Party, which resulted in the punishment and/or dismissal of the managers and Party officials Zinkevich exposes. Afterwards, Zinkevich was transferred to another state farm where she was rewarded with adequate housing, something all Soviet citizens struggled to obtain.

For a long time I have been a regular *Pravda* reader, but I am writing to you now, dear editors, for the first time. I earnestly ask you: what should I do next, how can I go on?

G. Zinkevich, "Who to Keep in Step With?" *Pravda*, October 26, 1981, p. 3.

First of all a few personal words about myself. I have a higher education, I have two children, I am a party member, I have worked for 25 years—and for 11 I was chief economist at the Kalinin state farm. I was a member of the People's Control group, a propagandist, a deputy to the village soviet, a delegate at party and trade union conferences.

Now directly about the matter which has persuaded me to write to the paper—and about the farm where I worked. Once it was an advanced farm, it made 1½ million rubles profit during the Ninth Five-year Plan. But then the profit turned into a deficit, and the Tenth Five-year Plan ended with big losses. They say that this was to do with various 'objective' reasons. But I considered then and still consider that it was due to poor management, an irresponsible attitude by the managers to their work, a lack of the necessary educational work with people.

I could not accept this. I exposed shortcomings at meetings of the buro of economic analysis, and named the people responsible. The director of the state farm N. Gruzinskii, who took over a successful farm and then started spoiling things, did not like this. And later, when I informed the People's Control organs about some disgraceful matters, other managers were displeased too.

Encountering Resistance

They quickly organised an attack on me. First they took me off the housing list on the quiet, and I lost my place in the queue for flats, and then all of a sudden I was dismissed. I was obliged to appeal to the republic People's Control Committee. I was reinstated. Then the director approached the matter differently: he closed the planning department, and transferred all its work to me alone, ordered the secretary not to type material on planning questions, prevented the accounting department from giving me material for analysis, prohibited my attending meetings with workers on the farm. For two years I was not given the leave due to me, and if eventually I got it, it was through the procuracy. More than once I and my children were evicted from our 17 square metres room in a hostel which was temporarily allocated to us while waiting for permanent housing. The humanity of our laws each time enabled me and my family to return. Then my rent was increased. . . .

Let me add to this that N. Gruzinskii himself lived for four years in a many-roomed government flat with all comforts, while a private home was being built for him, and during all this time he didn't pay a single kopek in rent . . . not a kopek for the use of electricity, which the chief accountant wrote off as a farm expense. Now Gruzinskii lives in his two-storey brick house with a brick barn, a cellar and a fence, built by casual workers *[shabashniki]* who had been hired to put up production units.

The director built himself an expensive house. But I am not writing this out of envy. It is painful to think that the summer camp for livestock that he started building was never put into use and is now broken up. The disinfectant bath, the annex to the farm hostel, etc. are also unfinished, and bricks, concrete, asphalt, lime, timber for building them were written off. And all this was above the norms and without proper accounting, overstating the losses.

Superintendent V. Gorbenko and his wife Z. Gorbenko, a normsetter, drew up false work rosters for the *shabashniki*, which the director then authorised and the chief accountant V. Parniko signed. Gruzinskii hired a home help, whom Gorbenko put down on the roster as a building worker. On Gruzinskii's instructions the farm took on 'dead souls' who did no work but received money.

The deputy chief accountant M. Shatskaya paid out a large sum of money for a clearly phoney work roster, and when I made a fuss about it because if we went on like that the whole farm would be robbed, she was allowed to give in her own notice. O. Gruzinskaya, the director's wife, an inspector in the cadres department, forged Shatskaya's workbook, giving her an uninterrupted work record when in fact there had been several interruptions. The head of the pig farm M. Dovgo was short of 262 centners [28,880 pounds, or more than 14 tons] of meat on 1 January 1978. Gruzinskii and his wife drew up a voluntary discharge. Tons of meat were falsely written off, as if the meat had spoilt. Farm horses were sold off to some scoundrels. . . .

The Whistleblower Tries Again

In sum, the list of the most various abuses could be extended. I informed the district party committee and the republic Ministry of Food about them. My letters were sent back to the same place where these things had occurred, and there they 'drew conclusions', 'took measures'—they evicted my children from the hostel, and generally covered me with dirt. They even expelled me from the party. As they say, I was 'put under expulsion'.

I appealed to the province party committee. Thanks to the head of the agricultural department A. Kikot', instructor M. Gashchenko and other comrades, who took an honest attitude to this matter, my party card was returned to me. The province soviet of people's deputies restored me to my place in the housing queue.

After this my submission to the investigative organs concerning the squandering of socialist property, about which I had earlier told the district party committee, was confirmed. The farm director Gruzinskii was removed from his post, and criminal charges were brought against the culprits.

The general director of the Belotserkov production agricultural canning association, to which our farm is subordinated, appointed a new director, M. Mandzyuk. But he had evidently already adopted the appropriate attitude, because he immediately began looking for various 'blemishes' in my work, and wrote a number of statements about me to the association. After that one directive after another descended on me . . . and now I have been dismissed again.

Yes, I would like to tell you about another matter. It was established that the former director Gruzinskii and his friends overpaid the *shabashniki* by 25,709 rubles, which brought the farm a significant loss. True, the Belotserkov procuracy issued a resolution pardoning them under the amnesty. The resolution was sent to the district party committee, so that those communists guilty of criminal acts would be penalised through party channels. From there it was sent to the farm, to the primary party organisation. And what happened? At the party meeting not a word was said against the former director and his friends.

The Whistleblower Is Attacked Again

The meeting restricted itself to a discussion about Gruzinskii and his circle. The district party committee changed this decision because of its lack of principle. But this was later. On that day I again got into trouble. The new party secretary V. Genailo (related by blood to the 'circle'), who was sent to us from outside, declared that he was going to expel me from the party and kick me out of my job; he abused me personally although I am old enough to be his mother. The director V. Mandzyuk supported him, and threw all the village gossip at me.

What for? I cannot understand what motivated the party secretary who had worked on the farm and in his party position for 21 days. I cannot understand what motivated the director. Sometimes he made demands on me that were apparently correct, but then himself turned out to be dishonest. After his appointment to the post of director V. Mandzyuk illegally received 500 rubles travelling expenses and returned them to the till only after a year, following inspection.

They say that I am an unsociable person, that I am nervous, that I can lose control and be rude. I admit that it happens. And afterwards, if I feel that I was wrong, I apologise. I have been criticised and penalised through party channels for this. But not once has anyone asked why it happens. With 25 years of service and 11 years working at the farm, I still have not obtained normal housing conditions and am still living with my children in the hostel. Meanwhile, V. Usmanov, someone who came to the farm from goodness knows where, a lover of spirits and a former party secretary, was given a five-room detached house for a family of two. Gorbenko also got a similar detached house. Neither of them now work at the farm but they have retained their homes. The new party secretary V. Genailo has also been allocated a six-room cottage. And these people say to me: be polite. . . .

Chief accountant V. Parnikoza, in spite of her financial 'tricks', stayed on as chief accountant at the farm, but now with a personal supplement to her salary, and now she lectures me: I suffered all these misfortunes because I 'didn't keep in step'. Gruzinskaya is still working in her post, also with a raise. Her husband, the former director of the farm, was appointed by general director Pavlov as head of the transport shop of the association. And they want me to smile at them?

They certainly 'keep in step'. But I do not want to and cannot do that. True, I once gave in and did them a favour. I helped the director to issue an illegal instruction transferring some farm machine operators who were working on the harvest to another grade, giving them somewhat higher wages. But I don't commend myself for this. My father, an invalid of the Great Patriotic War, taught me another way. My older sister, whose work in the years of post-war ruin was rewarded with a Gold Star and two Orders of Lenin, also taught me another way.

No, I am not able to engage in deceitful methods of planning, which my former managers constantly demanded of me. I cannot lie—draw up a plan understating the weight of cattle and pigs, and artificially understating the production of milk, meat and vegetables. This path of deceiving the government has been chosen by our association and by some other farms in the district. Last year we had millions of rubles losses. . . .

Five years ago I passed a course of higher education in Odessa with distinction. Two years ago I passed a reassessment at the farm with distinction. And now it appears, I am a good-for-nothing specialist, a poor worker. . . .

From the Editors

When G. Zinkevich's letter was already at the printers, she wrote to us again: 'On my request, instructor M. Gashchenko from the agricultural department of Kiev province party committee again paid a visit. As a result I was fixed up with a similar post in another farm.

But what concerns me is this: why don't we struggle enough with those who behave illegally, who abuse their positions, pursue only their own interests? People tell me in such cases that our state is massive—that you can't keep an eye on everyone. I disagree with this point of view.'

As we see, a person who insists on our principles comes into sharp conflict with her colleagues. What is their position? What is the position of the party organisation, the district party committee? This is what needs to be seriously discussed, and needs to be evaluated in a principled way. It is a question of the duty of a party member in the struggle against shortcomings.

Troubleshooting in the Tire Industry

Nikita S. Khrushchev

Virtually every manufactured item was in short supply in the Soviet Union prior to World War II. Since demand far exceeded supply, it was necessary for factories to produce as much as they could as fast as they could. Workers who exceeded their individual production quotas received special recognition and access to rare consumer goods. Managers whose factories exceeded their overall quotas were promoted into the upper echelons of the Communist Party. Consequently, workers and managers were constantly looking for shortcuts that would increase production.

Nikita S. Khrushchev was first secretary of the Communist Party of the Soviet Union from 1953 to 1964. In 1939, the year the incident in this selection occurred, he was first secretary of the Ukrainian Party Central Committee, in effect the governor of the Ukraine. Here he sheds light on the deleterious effect high production quotas had on quality. He also demonstrates one of the fundamental problems with Soviet industry, that crucial production decisions were often made by party bosses who knew next to nothing about manufacturing.

For a period before the war, members of the Politbureau and Central Committee were forbidden to fly in airplanes. This started after [Anastas I.] Mikoyan [the Politbureau's specialist on trade] let some pilot take him for a joyride in Belorussia. The incident was written up in the

Nikita S. Khrushchev, *Khrushchev Remembers*, translated and edited by Strobe Talbott. Boston: Little, Brown and Company, 1970.

newspapers. When Stalin read that one of his men had been up in a plane doing all sorts of aerobatics, he gave Mikoyan a stern dressing down and promptly made a rule that Central Committee members and first secretaries of the Republics weren't allowed in airplanes. I was fairly disappointed because I loved to fly. For a while I either had to take the train between Kiev and Moscow or else drive.

Aleksandr Georgievich Zhuravlev was my chauffeur for almost thirty-three years. My children used to call him Uncle Sasha. He was good at his job, and he liked it, too. I respected and trusted him.

A Problem with Tires

During a trip from Kiev to Moscow in 1939, Aleksandr Georgievich told me that the tires which were being issued for our cars were wearing out much too quickly. In fact, they were blowing out at the sides while they were still almost brand-new. When I got to Moscow, I told Stalin that this manufacturing defect was costing us a lot of time and money.

Stalin never liked to hear anyone criticize something that was Soviet-made. He listened to my complaint with obvious displeasure. Then he angrily instructed me to liquidate this situation and to find the culprits. He said, "So you're criticizing our tire industry, too? Everyone's criticizing it. We are going to instruct you to deal with this situation yourself. You are going to look into it and recommend the measures necessary to eradicate these defects and to ensure the issue of good-quality tires from our factories."

I answered, "Comrade Stalin, I would accept this assignment with pleasure, but I'm absolutely unfamiliar with the rubber industry and tire manufacturing. I've had something to do with the coal industry, with metallurgy, and with the construction business, but the tire industry is completely unfamiliar to me."

"So familiarize yourself. Take over immediately. You won't go back to the Ukraine until you've taken care of this problem."

A resolution was drawn up establishing a commission, and

I was confirmed as chairman of it. I was a bit worried. I didn't know how much time it would take, and I didn't know if I would be able to cope with the problem. I convened the commission and summoned specialists from the Yaroslavl* tire factory, from Leningrad, from Moscow, and from various ministries. With the help of the Central Committee apparatus, I collected everyone who knew anything about tire manufacturing. Our consultations took place in the Central Committee building. Everyone had a chance to give his views. I remember that the director of the Yaroslavl factory made a particularly good impression on me from the start.

After the first round of consultations I reported to Stalin what everyone had said and then offered my own considerations. Stalin said, "I suggest you go to Yaroslavl and work this out on the spot. The Yaroslavl tire factory is the best we have."

So I went to Yaroslavl. I took some of the specialists with me from Moscow. The Secretary of the Regional Party Committee was Comrade Patolichev, who many years later became Minister of Foreign Trade. The Chairman of the Regional Executive Committee was a young Armenian who, like Patolichev, was a metallurgical engineer. They both made a good impression on me. As soon as I arrived, I told them why I had come to Yaroslavl and asked them to give me their help.

First of all, I wanted to see how the rubber outer covering of the tires was made. I told the director of the factory, "Don't describe your whole operation to me now. That would be a waste of time. Just lead me along your assembly line. I want to start from scratch." I reviewed the whole assembly line, lingering here and there and watching any workers who were doing something that interested me. I didn't have time to see the vulcanization process, so I relied on the specialists who were reporting to me to fill me in on that subject.

I was particularly interested in the technique by which the

* Yaroslavl is a city in Russia; it is hundreds of miles from the Ukraine, Khrushchev's bailiwick.

workers applied the wire cords to the tires. I watched them for a long time. They did this deftly and quickly, not even looking at their hands as they worked. Their hands moved like musicians' hands. I admired them and later asked about the production plans for what they were doing. I was told how many layers of wire cording were applied and what purpose the cords served. On the basis of what I was told, I sensed that I had found the weak spot. I had seen how quickly the workers applied the cords, and I knew that they had to be applied and stretched evenly, so that all the strands in each layer would work together like a single strand. If the cords were applied evenly, you could multiply the durability of one strand by the total number of strands and that would be the resistance of the whole layer to rupture. However, if a layer were applied unevenly, each strand would work by itself and the cords would be torn one by one. That's why the tires were breaking down. There were other problems, too, but this was the main one.

I called over the director of the factory. "Comrade Mitrokhin, let me see the instruction manual you're using for the manufacture of tires. I want to see what sort of production process is recommended. Since we purchased the equipment for this plant from America, the Americans must have recommended a process for us to use."

"Yes, we have all the instructions."

"Then check those instructions against the process now being used and report to me exactly what changes have been made in the recommended process."

According to Mitrokhin's report, there had indeed been some departures from the instructions recommended by the American firm. One or two layers of cording had been eliminated since it was thought that the number left would be sufficient to guarantee durability. I was also told that the amount of reinforcing wire had been diminished at the edges. One or two rings had been taken out. All this had been done to make the whole process more economical. I knew immediately we had found the bug.

"When were these changes made?" I asked.

"Comrade [Lazar M.] Kaganovich came here to make an inspection tour and studied our production methods. He recommended these changes." This had been when Kaganovich was head of the People's Commissariat of Transport. Apparently he had brought Sergo Ordzhonikidze [Commissar for Heavy Industry] with him to Yaroslavl.

"All right," I said, "give me the official minutes of your meeting with Kaganovich so that I can report to Comrade Stalin and the Central Committee. Now you should start following exactly the production method used in America." During my tour around the factory I'd notice that in this one, as in any factory, there was an honor board with the photographs of the best producers or, as they were called, the shock-workers. I asked the manager of the factory, "How does the productivity of your workers compare with that of the workers in America who apply tire cording?" I was told that we had made a giant step forward and had surpassed the American workers.

The Problem Is Solved

We prepared a draft resolution based on our findings, and I returned to Moscow. When I reported to Stalin, I stressed that we were producing poor-quality tires because, in our desire to economize, we had violated the production procedure recommended by the firm from which the equipment was purchased. We had "corrected" the American manufacturers and "improved" the production process, but as a result, one of their tires lasted ten times as long as one of ours. That certainly is economizing for you!

Then I told Stalin that I considered it a mistake to try to raise the productivity and output norms too high. We should avoid trying to economize on production and to raise productivity at the expense of quality. The tire workers may have surpassed their quota, but they had overdone it. Our workers should have been encouraged to pay more attention to quality when applying the tire cording. In order to do that, we needed to lower their output norms. We were learning that if you aim for a level of productivity which deprives a worker of a chance to do quality work, the product will be spoiled. All the shock-workers on the honor board at the factory were, in actual fact, ruining what they produced, lowering the productivity of our drivers, and preventing us from getting efficient use out of our motor pool.

Stalin listened to me attentively. I could see he was terribly irritated by what I was telling him, and I understood why. Any man who cares for the welfare of the State—especially the man who holds the leading position in the State—ought well to have been disturbed by this kind of news. Stalin said, "I agree with you. Give us your recommendations and we will approve them."

In my report I introduced recommendations that output norms be lowered, that workers' wage rates be raised, and that a whole series of other measures be taken as suggested by the specialists from the factory, from the scientific research institutes, and from the People's Commissariats.

Stalin then said, "We must pass a resolution to discourage excessive competition for quantity over quality among the workers by prohibiting the posting of honor boards at the tire factory."

On general principle I would have been against this. It had always been a Leninist contention that competition is a healthy thing for productivity, and productivity is the bedrock of industrial development. However, I approved of Stalin's position in this particular case.

I was pleased that with the help of the specialists, I had succeeded in pinpointing and liquidating the weak spot in the manufacture of tires. We sensed at the time that we were heading toward war, and in wartime the mobility of the army depends on the quality of the transport industry. I was pleased that as soon as we liquidated the defects and restored proper production methods, high-quality durable tires started to be issued. We conducted tests at various factories to see how long tires could last without repair. If the results of the test were positive, a factory would receive a prize which went to all the workers collectively for their contribution to the general good.

Shortly afterward, Mitrokhin, the director of the Yaroslavl factory, became Commissar of the Chemical Industry. I was pleased that Stalin hadn't forgotten my high recommendation of this man and had assigned him to such a responsible post.

In relation to the scale of our whole manufacturing industry, this episode concerned a minor matter, but it still had its significance for me. I've told this story to illustrate how Stalin was sometimes capable of a conscientious and statesmanly approach to problems. He was a jealous lord and master of the State, and he fought against bureaucracy and corruption and defects of all kinds. He was a great man, a great organizer and a leader, but he was also a despot. He often fought with harsh methods against the primitiveness which still afflicted our industry. In his desire to look out for the welfare of the State, he was merciless in liquidating any defect that came to his attention. But it shouldn't be forgotten that as a despot, Stalin also did much harm, especially in his treatment of the Party and military leadership. This was all a result of his unhealthy mistrust of other people.

We still have problems of productivity and output. You have probably seen on more than one occasion how men and women are engaged in chipping ice off the pavement with crowbars. This is unproductive labor. Such a sight really makes one uncomfortable. So much has been done in our country to mechanize complicated production processes, so many machines have been created to make work easier, and the first artificial earth satellites have been developed, but as for replacing the crowbar and shovel with a machine—we have not yet gotten around to that. We pay too little attention to such matters and regard them as trivial. But is this trivial? No, it is "trivial matters" like this that constitute the work of many people.

Boosting Worker Productivity Through Sports

Yuri Brokhin

Yuri Brokhin was a Soviet mining engineer and filmmaker who immigrated to the United States in 1972. In this selection from his first book, he describes how the first secretary of the Voroshilovgrad region increased industrial output during the 1960s by building a championship soccer team. His story shows the importance of soccer, the Soviet Union's most popular spectator sport, to workers who had little else to cheer about. It also gives some indication as to how the Communist Party promoted and demoted its leaders, and the important role of bribery in making communism work.

In 1972, for the first time in the history of Soviet sports, the Voroshilovgrad soccer team, Sunrise, became the national champs. The sensational victory of the provincial Ukrainian soccer team, which literally smashed its famous Russian opponents, made Soviet sports history.

For long afterward, in newspapers and magazines, on radio and television, at seminars and conferences, there were discussions about the coach's tactical innovations, the players' psychological prepping, and the unexpectedly bold technical maneuvres.

But not a single publication or a single public meeting ever mentioned the name of the man who had actually

Yuri Brokhin, *Hustling on Gorky Street: Sex and Crime in Russia Today*, translated by E.B. Kane and Yuri Brokhin. New York: Dial Press, 1975.

brought about the miracle. This man was not meant to play the role of a sports czar. He never appeared on the stadium's grassy field during a game. He was never seen in a coach's uniform, or holding a ball, or in soccer shoes. But everyone in Voroshilovgrad, young and old, knew that the real creator and inspirer of the victory was none other than—First Secretary of the Voroshilovgrad Communist Party Committee, Vladimir Shevchenko. . . .

In the spring of 1961, . . . Voroshilovgrad received a new boss of Party mafia. The mafia captains, lieutenants, and soldiers christened their new boss "Shef" ("Chief"), using the first syllable of his name: Shev—pronounced "shef"—chenko.

The Soccer Bug

In accordance with tradition, Shef called a Party plenary meeting and delivered his inaugural address, which said in part:

"The Party Committee Bureau is of the opinion that the distribution of season tickets to soccer games is a correct continuation of the struggle for power to the Soviets!"

Nobody asked why. The Party activists, who till then had struggled for Soviet power on the coal front, the steelworking front, the corn front, and the peaceful-coexistence front, discovered volcanoes of soccer passion in their souls.

Management heads with well-attuned ears quickly grabbed money intended for hospitals, schools, and apartment houses and plunked down a magnificent suburban training camp, named Bedryagina Dacha. Every mining supervisor and factory director was called in to swear fidelity to Shef and to promise to bring in his monthly donation for the team.

The soccer bug bit statisticians and economists. The computers began printing out data on the correlation between goals for, goals against, and labor productivity.

The epidemic reached the confectionary and liquor industries, resulting in soccer candies, soccer-ball cakes, stadium cocktails, and goalie liqueurs.

And although the first few years brought no perceptible results, Shevchenko never tired of emphasizing that soccer was not just a one-shot campaign: It was for real, and it was for always. . . .

For a week before any scheduled local game, the Party Committee resembled an ocean liner entering a storm belt. Data about coal and steel production were no longer brought to Shef's desk. Instead, he was brought charts of the progress of the teams in competition for the all-Union soccer championship.

Shef's first deputy analyzed the number of broken ribs and black eyes on the opposing team. The second deputy did research on which of the enemy players could be bribed. . . .

Game Day

On the day of a game, the central reviewing box of the stadium resembled a ballroom of the Waldorf Astoria. The spectators came chicly dressed. The women wore Japanese banlon dresses (considered the height of world fashion), and the men wore made-to-order suits from the best tailor in town (slightly Pierre Cardin, mostly Brooklyn garment maker).

Waiting for the game to begin, the ladies and gentlemen crunched sunflower seeds. VIP mouths spat out shells on less-VIP heads. But the latter bore it in silence.

To the left and right of the reviewing stand sat middle-caliber officials. They modestly drank lemonade, for this was in the pre-détente days when Pepsi-Cola was considered equivalent to poison.

And all the remaining seats were occupied by the working class. They were solid, in the sense that there was not a single pair of pants among them without a bottle in one pocket.

Many drooled from thirst, but they waited. The director of the stadium was announcing over the loudspeaker:

"Dear soccer fans! Here are some of the results of the last game played in this stadium. Steelworker Grishin, in an intoxicated state, raped a woman student from the Pedagogical Institute. The court has sentenced him to fifteen years' imprisonment. Coal miner Filinov, in an intoxicated state, put out the eye of the soccer fan sitting next to him. Seven years imprisonment. A group of workers staged a mass fist-fight after the last game. Armed with bottles of vodka, they succeeded in breaking a considerable number of one another's skulls. The result: 210 men are in the hospital, and about 100 have received jail terms ranging from one to five years. And that's the news, friends. Enjoy the game!"

Then followed the strains of the soccer march, the game began, and the workers, having paid their respects to solidarity and sympathy with suffering co-workers, proceeded to down vodka straight from the bottle.

As soon as the forward of the Sunrise team made a goal, the whole stadium leaped up with a howl of victory and turned—not in the direction of the soccer player, but in the direction of Shef. As if his hands held the levers that controlled the players' legs, and only he, by his skillful manipulations, could pull the pail of money out from under the slot machine.

Shef smiled, and applauded in return. The unity of Party and people was in full evidence.

Shef Asserts His Power

Dima Durdenko was the team's best forward. He was pestered by autograph hunters like a real star, and he was paid more than the others: 600 rubles a month. . . .

One day Durdenko missed a goal in a decisive match. After the game, some members of the Party Committee Bureau gathered in the locker room, wearing dispirited, gloomy faces. I went, too. Shevchenko soon appeared.

"Dima," he said. "It is the basic principle of socialism: From each according to his ability, to each according to his work."

With this explanation, the boss began to punch the player in the face, cold-bloodedly and precisely.

On one side, the beating was observed by the members of the Committee Bureau.

On the other side were Dima's wet, dirty teammates who had just come in from the field.

And all were silent. I too was silent.

And this silence was more terrible than the bloody beating. . . .

In mid-1964, Vladimir Shcherbitsky, Party leader of the whole Ukraine and therefore Shevchenko's boss as well, lost his post as a result of criticizing [First Secretary Nikita] Khrushchev. True, Shcherbitsky, who enjoyed wide respect, was let off lightly, merely being reassigned to his old post as First Secretary of the Party organization in Dnepropetrovsk.

Passing through Voroshilovgrad, the fallen Shcherbitsky decided to stop and pay a visit to his old colleague Shevchenko. A secretary informed him that Shevchenko was "very busy right now."

It was a deliberate act of disdain. Shevchenko sweetened his life by spitting in the faces of former leaders and colleagues. He based his behavior on the historical experience of Soviet politicians, particularly bloody Stalin, who climbed to the top on a mountain of his comrades' corpses. This experience told Shevchenko: The harder you spit, the farther you'll go. . . .

The Team Flounders

Despite all efforts, the playing of the Sunrise team left much to be desired. They barely dragged themselves to a place somewhere in the middle of the league, then fell back to last place again, and were even threatened with being thrown out of the major league altogether.

After a profound analysis of the situation, Shevchenko reached a conclusion: "We need a Jew!" Not in the role of coach, but in the role of talent scout. The Jew was found. He was Chaim Mishalsky. Chaim was inducted into Christianity, appointed a section chief in the Party Committee, and given a "straight Russian" passport (since a Party Committee member's passport could hardly have contained the word "Jew").*

Equipped with unlimited cash, Chaim Mishalsky set out

* Like the tsarist government it replaced, the Communist Party was virulently anti-Semitic, as this passage makes clear.

on his travels to buy up soccer legs and coach heads.

Soviet soccer regulations allow for only one month—December—when players are permitted to transfer from one team to another. This is the so-called soccer honeymoon. But it is run like the annual year-end sale at Macy's: a lot of noise and dust, but not much merchandise to be had. The big soccer patrons (Party bosses) keep the famous stars under virtual house arrest, while promising rookies are simply sent to the Army for a month's "special training."

In order to get a good product, one has to go to unusual lengths. Mishalsky went to such lengths. . . .

One day, out of the clear blue sky, Yosif Sabo, best forward on the Kiev team, the Dynamos, announced that he was too tired to go on with his soccer career. Efforts were made to dissuade him from quitting. He was bullied and cajoled, but remained adamant. There was nothing left to do but give him a hero's send-off at the Kiev stadium. One hundred thousand fans gave him his final "hurrah!" The illustrious forward stood in silent farewell, tears rolling down his cheeks.

Soon, a black government limousine appeared on the streets of Voroshilovgrad. But no government official rode inside. On the back seat, there was only the former Dynamo soccer champ, Yosif Sabo. His legs were worth 15,000 rubles. He could also hit the goal corners with his head quite well, so another 15,000 was thrown in. . . .

A soccer player named Tsapun was another achievement of Mishalsky's. Tsapun was kidnapped right out of a stadium locker room. Since he had been the best offensive player on the neighboring Donetsk team, the Miners, his capture was doubly valuable.

Tsapun understood well enough that he would be paid a great deal more money on the Sunrise team. But being a quick-witted lad, he wanted to rip off as juicy a piece of bounty as possible. He announced categorically that he would not go out on any soccer field until the following conditions were met: 1) His pop, a Donetsk hairdresser, had to be given his own beauty salon in the center of Voroshilovgrad; 2) his kid brother, under a ten-year prison sentence for armed robbery, had to be released.

A fashionable private hairdressing salon, though not precisely a socialist institution, was equipped and opened in the center of Voroshilovgrad in two weeks. But springing the young holdup man from a prison in another town proved to be more complicated. For this operation, Shef sent General Troshchenko, section chief of the Voroshilovgrad KGB, to Donetsk. The general informed the Donetsk police that a matter of particular state security required that prisoner Tsapun be brought in for a confrontation with his co-conspirators in Voroshilovgrad. Suspecting nothing, the Donetsk authorities complied. On the road to Voroshilovgrad, a well-simulated "escape" by the younger Tsapun, who "fled

The Problem of Sluggishness

Mikhail Gorbachev was named general secretary of the Communist Party in 1985; as such, he was the Soviet Union's last leader. He attempted to save Soviet communism via the policies of glasnost (openness) and perestroika (restructuring). In this excerpt from his 1987 book, he identifies one of the major difficulties in making communism work.

There is also the problem of sluggishness, of inertia. The practice of waiting for instructions from above on every matter, of relying on top-level decisions has not yet been done away with. Not that this is surprising, for this is the way it used to be from workshops to ministries, and it is still having its effect today, even in the upper echelons of administration. The point is that people grew unaccustomed to thinking and acting in a responsible and independent way. . . . The greatest difficulty in our restructuring effort lies in our thinking, which has been molded over the past years. Everyone, from General Secretary to worker, has to alter this thinking.

Mikhail Gorbachev, *Perestroika: New Thinking for Our Country and the World.* New York: Harper & Row, 1987, p. 65.

in an unknown direction," took place. To be sure, a couple of years later, when the elder Tsapun stopped making goals, the younger was quickly apprehended and returned to his Donetsk cell.

How much was paid to the former coach of the Soviet national team, Konstantin Beskov, remained a secret. But the simple fact that Mishalsky managed to get such a man caused a sensation in Voroshilovgrad. . . .

At that time, Beskov (who is now once again the coach for the Soviet national team) had recently lost his job after the national team's defeat by Spain in the European finals. Being a clever man as well as a talented coach, Beskov understood perfectly well what it meant to work with a soccer team under the constant watch of a fanatical Party boss.

Naturally, Shef hesitated to hit him in the teeth. But Beskov couldn't plan a single combination without Shef's consent. And during the game, players were replaced not at Beskov's, but at Shef's command.

If Sunrise won, Shevchenko would phone Beskov and say: "Kostya, believe me, one of these days I'll make you lifetime coach of the national team." Shef seriously believed that sooner or later, he himself would reach the Kremlin.

But in 1966, Beskov could not achieve the desired results, and Shef dropped him. The same thing happened with the coaches who followed. He hired miracle workers, capable of raising castles out of thin air. But his own pigheaded tyranny and unrestraint, like a monstrous machine, destroyed his own dreams. . . .

Raising Money to Support the Team

Sometimes [Nikolai] Shuvalov [one of Shevchenko's lieutenants] took me along on trips to the mines. Questions of installing new mining equipment were the least of his worries. He had to find money to support the soccer team. In contrast to the professional players in decadent bourgeois sports, Soviet players are considered amateurs. At each mine, a soccer player was supposedly employed as an ore-car driver, a drill operator, or whatever. Naturally, no soccer halfback or forward ever saw the inside of a coal mine. But they had to receive 150 rubles a month for their operation of mining equipment. And since market prices for soccer legs in the Soviet union were skyrocketing, Shuvalov had to order the mine foremen to exaggerate the number of miners considerably. The poor supervisors had to invent workers who were capable of operating five machines at a time, for which they were paid five salaries a month.

After a visit to the mines, Shuvalov's car looked like a cross between a larder and a bank office. The trunk was crammed with vodka, cheese, sausage, black and red caviar, and smoked fish. The back seat was covered with paper packets, big and little envelopes, and bundles wrapped in newspaper. All contained the same thing: money. I don't know exactly what Shuvalov received the bribes for. Most probably, just so he would "live and let live." Translated, this means, "steal and let steal": accept bonuses for yet-uninvented inventions, manipulate accounts, and most important, add digits to the figures for coal production.

For example, a mine may have a monthly quota of 50,000 tons of coal. If 52,000 tons are mined, then everybody, from the lowest worker to the highest superior, will receive a bonus of 30 to 40 percent of his or her monthly salary. Naturally, if the mine is not in a position to produce these superquota tons, they will be extracted from wherever possible, but not from underground. At best, the coal will be bought from wealthier neighbors, and at worst, figures will be changed, so that paper tons are produced.

Later, I learned that Shuvalov divided the bribes with Shef. Shef in turn probably greased someone over him. If this long, multirunged ladder ever broke down, with it would disappear the chief stimulus to labor—the bribe. It would be the end of the Soviet national economy. . . .

In the Prague summer of 1968, [when Soviet military forces put down an uprising in Czechoslovakia, Khruschev's successor, Leonid] Brezhnev let the world know that any ideas whatsoever are easily crushed under the treads of tanks. The cult of the new leader dates from that time. One of the first things that Brezhnev did was to return Shcherbitsky to his former post as Party boss of the Ukraine. Such a resurrection was extremely rare among Communist apparatchiks [Party bureaucrats]. It happened because Shcherbitsky was a protégé of Brezhnev and one of the most respected members of the Dnepropetrovsk Party . . . which was founded by Brezhnev in 1947, when he was Party Secretary of Dnepropetrovsk. . . .

In 1970, Vladimir Shcherbitsky was elevated to the Politburo and thereby became a member of the chief decision-making body of the country.

It is not known what Shcherbitsky personally thought of Shevchenko. But I know for a fact that Shevchenko himself immediately felt the ground slide under his feet. The spit globs of 1964 turned into uncomfortable presentiments of counterpunches.

The Connection Between Winning Soccer and Higher Production

Shef staked his last card: soccer. Not that he was any kind of gambler. His soccer passion was combined with a politician's calculations. In order to understand the relationship between soccer and politics, one must know what Voroshilovgrad Oblast [a political division of a state] was in the industrial balance of the Soviet Union.

Voroshilovgrad Oblast: 15 percent of the coal, 60 percent of the diesel locomotives, 10 percent of the iron and steel, and 30 percent of the chemical industry of the Soviet Union. Tens of thousands of workers are employed by the enterprises of this gigantic industrial complex.

What does the average worker have, besides his salary of 150 rubles ($200) a month?

The opportunity of providing himself with food, meaning he can go into a store and buy yellowed sausage or cans of ancient sardines in tomato sauce.

The opportunity of free weekends, meaning he can get drunk on vodka and fight with his wife, who is embittered by a lack of money and a surplus of children.

The opportunity of entertainment, meaning he can turn on the television and listen to a nauseating recitative about building the happy future.

The opportunity of showing a Communist attitude toward his work, meaning he can go to the mine or factory at 6 A.M., sweat seven sweats, and uncomplainingly receive peanuts.

In other words, it is no bed of roses. And suppose this "no bed of roses" goes on for years? Eventually, this worker will start asking What is this? and Why?, wondering about his life and the life of others like him. And the next thing you know, he will begin smashing all the magnificent equipment and assembly lines.

Shef, a psychologist and a strategist, always took these possibilities, these "opportunities" into account. He pushed soccer because it was the only fresh, naturally edible dish available. It was a great modern assembly, where a worker could forget life's futility and hardships, drink a bottle of vodka with friends, let some passions out of his soul, and feel like a worthy member of a roaring herd. Suddenly, life felt easier to the working man.

And as a matter of fact, it was no joke: The computers determined that every time the Sunrise team won a local game, there was about a 50 percent jump in the productivity of the factories and mines of Voroshilovgrad.

As long as the country received a steady flow of crucial products, it was not so simple to throw out of power the man who kept this flow going.

In 1972, alarmed for his future, Shef decided to step on the neck of his own emotions. He stopped interfering in the training and tactics of the Sunrise team. All authority was completely given over to a new coach, German Zonin.

Shef concentrated his energy upon financial matters exclusively. Using cutthroat techniques, he forced the mine supervisors to pay each soccer player about $1,200 a month—an unheard-of salary in Soviet soccer. . . .

Chaim Mishalsky took care of the umpires. To his surprise, an umpire would be told that he had a deluxe room in a hotel. No less surprisingly, when he arrived, there would be a couple of thousand rubles under his pillow. And if he justified the hopes that were placed in him, he could go home looking from side to side, fully expecting to see a nice new car waiting for him around the corner—or at the very least, a piano.

Shevchenko's appointment of his own protégé, Boris Zenchenko, to the post of Director of the Soccer Commission of the USSR was the crowning achievement . . . of the Voroshilovgrad Party. . . .

The Scam Revealed

On the night of November 21, 1972, the residents of Voroshilovgrad were awakened by the explosions and lights of a grandiose fireworks display. The Sunrise team had become soccer champions of the Soviet Union. Shef attained inner peace and his former self-confidence. He did not suspect that the blade of the Party guillotine already hung over his head.

The factoids (to borrow a word from Norman Mailer) about Vladimir Shcherbitsky are that he is relatively honest, decent, and has not been just a yes-man, either under Khrushchev or Brezhnev. He is also no anti-Semite, either in words or deeds—a rare trait in a Party leader.

But he is, above all, a professional politician. And according to the rules of the game, softheartedness is equivalent to suicide. Shevchenko could not be forgiven for his past insolence, because he would consider Shcherbitsky a weakling, and would inevitably become a danger to Shcherbitsky later on.

On December 14, 1973, Shcherbitsky came to Voroshilovgrad for the showdown.

The following day, the government newspaper *Pravda of Ukrainia* published this announcement:

> For serious errors committed during leadership of the Oblast Party Committee, for violation of Leninist norms of Party life and the principles of collective leadership, for eyeglass wiping [= paper machinations], inefficiency, and wastefulness, Vladimir Shevchenko has been removed from his post as First Secretary of the Voroshilovgrad Oblast Party Committee.

All these resounding phrases of newspaper propaganda can be reduced to the simple words: He robbed them blind.

It is estimated in the West that Soviet Party and government bureaucrats manage to misappropriate the equivalent of $16 billion a year on the job. Similar figures are undoubtedly known to the Politburo.

Shevchenko evidently exceeded the standard norms of permissible theft. He overreached himself. But on top of that, he made a serious tactical error in his treatment of Shcherbitsky.

So what comes next—a trial, prison, confiscation of property, a loud newspaper campaign? Nothing of the sort. This powerful member of the Communist Party's Central Committee, head of the Voroshilovgrad Oblast Committee, deputy to the Supreme Soviet of the USSR, on December 15, 1973, simply became a nonperson.

There will never be a Watergate-style scandal in the Soviet Union. No Party boss ever has been or ever will be brought to trial and jailed for bribery, corruption, or theft. If one corrupt high official were ever sent to jail, all the rest would have to go too, almost without exception.

Overnight, Shef's liquidation broke the aggressive spirit of the Sunrise soccer team. The champions finished in next-to-last place in the 1974 season.

Chronology

1917
Bolsheviks (socialists loyal to Vladimir Lenin) seize control of the Russian government.

1918
The first Soviet constitution mandates separation of church and state. The Russian civil war begins between Bolsheviks (Reds) and non-Bolsheviks (Whites).

1920
The Russian civil war ends in a Bolshevik victory.

1922
The Union of Soviet Socialist Republics (Soviet Union) is formed.

1924
Lenin dies and is replaced by Josef Stalin.

1926
The Family Code reforms family life and divorce.

1927
The first Five-Year Plan is adopted.

1928
The first Five-Year Plan begins, focusing on revitalizing industry.

1929
Churches and religious associations are banned. The "cult

of personality" begins with the celebration of Stalin's fiftieth birthday.

1930
A program to collectivize agriculture begins.

1932
Famine breaks out in the Ukraine.

1933
The second Five-Year Plan begins, focusing on production of consumer goods.

1934
The Great Purge begins.

1935
The collectivization program is reformed.

1936
A new family law restricts abortion and divorce.

1938
The third Five-Year Plan begins, focusing on transforming the military.

1939
Soviets sign a nonaggression pact with Nazi Germany. The Soviet Union annexes eastern Poland.

1940
The Soviet Union annexes the Baltic States: Estonia, Latvia, and Lithuania.

1941
The "Great Patriotic War" begins when Nazis invade the Soviet Union.

1942
The Battle of Stalingrad is the turning point in the war in the East.

1943
Stalin eases restrictions on the Russian Orthodox Church.

1944
The Red Army drives the Germans out of the Soviet Union and invades Eastern Europe.

1945
The Red Army invades Germany. World War II ends.

1946
Persecution of intellectuals begins. Collectivization is reformed again.

1947
Famine breaks out in the Ukraine again.

1949
Soviets successfully test an atomic bomb.

1953
Stalin dies and is replaced by Nikita Khrushchev.

1954
The "virgin lands" program is adopted.

1956
De-Stalinization begins.

1957
Decentralization begins. Soviets launch the *Sputnik* satellite.

1958
A new penal code is adopted that abolishes "enemies of the state" as a criminal category.

1959
Soviets begin growing corn in the virgin lands.

1960
A U.S. spy plane (U2) is shot down over Soviet airspace.

1961
Soviets conduct the first successful manned spaceflight.

1962
The Cuban missile crisis brings the United States and the Soviet Union to the brink of war.

1963
The corn harvest fails.

1964
Khrushchev is removed from office and is replaced by Leonid Brezhnev and Aleksey Kosygin.

1965
Brezhnev begins undoing Khrushchev's reforms.

1972
SALT-I talks between the United States and the Soviet Union limit nuclear arms.

1977
Brezhnev becomes the top leader of the Soviet Union.

1979
SALT-II talks further limit nuclear arms.

1982
Brezhnev dies and is replaced by Yuri Andropov.

1984
Andropov dies and is replaced by Konstantin Chernenko.

1985
Chernenko dies and is replaced by Mikhail Gorbachev.

1986
The Chernobyl nuclear power plant disaster occurs.

1987
Perestroika implements economic reforms.

1988
The role of the Communist Party in Soviet affairs is reduced.

1989
Nationalist movements begin in the Baltic States.

1990
The Communist Party is split into factions over Gorbachev's reforms.

1991
Gorbachev resigns. The Soviet Union is dissolved.

For Further Research

Primary Sources

Yakov Alpert, *Making Waves: Stories from My Life.* New Haven, CT: Yale University Press, 2000.

Yuri Brokhin, *Hustling on Gorky Street: Sex and Crime in Russia Today.* New York: Dial, 1975.

William O. Douglas, *Russian Journey.* New York: Doubleday, 1956.

Barbara Alpern Engel and Anastasia Posadskaya-Vanderbeck, eds., *A Revolution of Their Own: Voices of Women in Soviet History.* Boulder, CO: Westview, 1998.

Mikhail Gorbachev, *Perestroika: New Thinking for Our Country and the World.* New York: Harper & Row, 1987.

Andrei Gromyko, *Memoirs.* New York: Doubleday, 1989.

Mary Halasz, with Piroska E. Kiss and Katalin E. Kiss, *From America with Love: Memoirs of an American Immigrant in the Soviet Union.* Boulder, CO: East European Monographs, 2000.

Susan Jacoby, *Moscow Conversations.* New York: Coward, McCann & Geoghegan, 1972.

Inez Cope Jeffery, *Inside Russia: The Life and Times of Zoya Zarubina.* Austin, TX: Eakin, 1999.

Alexandra Kollontai, *The Autobiography of a Sexually Emancipated Communist Woman.* New York: Herder and Herder, 1971.

Mary Mackler Leder, *My Life in Stalinist Russia: An American Woman Looks Back.* Bloomington: Indiana University Press, 2001.

Dmitry S. Likhachev, *Reflections on the Russian Soul: A Memoir.* New York: Central European University Press, 2000.

Nadezhda Mandelstam, *Hope Against Hope: A Memoir.* New York: Atheneum, 1970.

Nina Markovna, *Nina's Journey: A Memoir of Stalin's Russia and the Second World War.* Washington, DC: Regnery Gateway, 1989.

Nursultan Nazarbayev, *My Life, My Times, and the Future.* Northamptonshire, England: Pilkington, 1998.

Maya Plisetskaya, *I, Maya Plisetskaya.* New Haven, CT: Yale University Press, 2001.

Lewis H. Siegelbaum and Andrei Sokolov, eds., *Stalinism as a Way of Life: A Narrative in Documents.* New Haven, CT: Yale University Press, 2000.

Strobe Talbott, ed. and trans., *Khrushchev Remembers.* Boston: Little, Brown, 1970.

George R. Urban, ed., *Social and Economic Rights in the Soviet Bloc: A Documentary Review Seventy Years After the Bolshevik Revolution.* New Brunswick, NJ: Transaction Books, 1988.

Secondary Sources

Robert Conquest, *The Great Terror: A Reassessment.* New York: Oxford University Press, 1990.

R.W. Davies and Mark Harrison, eds., *The Economic Transformation of the Soviet Union, 1913–1945.* New York: Cambridge University Press, 1994.

Sheila Fitzpatrick, *Everyday Stalinism: Ordinary Life in Extraordinary Times: Soviet Russia in the 1930s.* New York: Oxford University Press, 1999.

———, *Stalin's Peasants: Resistance and Survival in the Russian Village After Collectivization.* New York: Oxford University Press, 1994.

Gregory L. Freeze, ed., *Russia: A History.* New York: Oxford University Press, 1997.

John L. Gaddis, *Russia, the Soviet Union, and the United States: An Interpretive History.* 2nd ed. New York: McGraw-Hill, 1990.

John G. Garrard and Carol Garrard, eds., *World War II and the Soviet People.* New York: St. Martin's, 1993.

J. Arch Getty and Roberta T. Manning, eds., *Stalinist Terror: New Perspectives.* New York: Cambridge University Press, 1993.

Graeme J. Gill, *The Origins of the Stalinist Political System.* New York: Cambridge University Press, 1990.

Wendy Z. Goldman, *Women, the State, and Revolution: Soviet Family Policy and Social Life, 1917–1936.* New York: Cambridge University Press, 1993.

Larry E. Holmes, *The Kremlin and the Schoolhouse: Reforming Education in Soviet Russia, 1917–1931.* Bloomington: Indiana University Press, 1991.

Geoffrey A. Hosking, *The First Socialist Society: A History of the Soviet Union from Within.* Cambridge, MA: Harvard University Press, 1993.

William B. Husband, *Revolution in the Factory: The Birth of the Soviet Textile Industry, 1917–1920.* New York: Oxford University Press, 1990.

John L.H. Keep, *Last of the Empires: A History of the Soviet Union, 1945–1991.* New York: Oxford University Press, 1995.

Peter Kenez, *Cinema and Soviet Society, 1917–1953.* New York: Cambridge University Press, 1992.

Martin E. Malia, *The Soviet Tragedy: A History of Socialism in Russia, 1917–1991.* New York: Free Press, 1994.

Mary McAuley, *Soviet Politics, 1917–1991.* New York: Oxford University Press, 1992.

Joseph L. Nogee and Robert H. Donaldson, *Soviet Foreign Policy Since World War II.* 4th ed. New York: Maxwell Macmillan International, 1992.

Alec Nove, *An Economic History of the USSR, 1917–1991.* New York: Penguin, 1992.

Robert Service, *Lenin: A Biography.* Cambridge, MA: Belknap, 2000.

Lewis H. Siegelbaum, *Soviet State and Society Between Revolutions, 1918–1929.* New York: Cambridge University Press, 1992.

Gerhard Simon, *Nationalism and Policy Towards the Nationalities in the Soviet Union: From Totalitarian Dictatorship to Post-Stalinist Society.* Boulder, CO: Westview, 1991.

Stephen White, *Gorbachev and After.* New York: Cambridge University Press, 1992.

Index